Sensible Mathematics

Sensible Mathematics

A GUIDE FOR

School Leaders

STEVEN LEINWAND

Heinemann
Portsmouth, NH

HEINEMANN

361 Hanover Street
Portsmouth, NH 03801–3912
www.heinemann.com

Offices and agents throughout the world

The author and publisher wish to thank those who have generously given permission to reprint borrowed material:

Figure 2-2: "Spiritual Revival?" by Anne R. Carey and Kevin Rechin from *USA Today*. Copyright 1998, *USA Today*. Reprinted with permission.

Figure 2-3: "Teen's Tobacco Choices" from *USA Today*. Copyright 1998, *USA Today*. Reprinted with permission.

Figure 2-5: "Medicaid's Bleak Future" by Grant Jerding from *USA Today*. Copyright 1998, *USA Today*. Reprinted with permission.

Page 12, "Cholesterol Pill May Help the Healthy" from *USA Today*. Copyright 1998, *USA Today*. Reprinted with permission.

Page 19, "Faulty Bridge Sign Traps Truck" from the *Waterbury Republican–American*, January 25, 1995. Reprinted with permission.

Figure 5-3: "Television Viewing Habits and Their Impact" from *A Guide to K-12 Program Development in Mathematics,* copyright 1999 by the Connecticut State Board of Education. Reprinted with permission.

James B. Adamson's letter to Thomas R. Kessell's class is reprinted by permission of Burger King Corporation. *(Continued on page vi)*

Library of Congress Cataloging-in-Publication Data

Leinwand, Steven.
    Sensible mathematics : a guide for school leaders / Steven Leinwand.
      p. cm.
    Includes bibliographical references.
    ISBN 0-325-00277-0 (alk. paper)
      1. Mathematics—Study and teaching.   2. Curriculum planning.   I. Title.
    QA11 .L45 2000
    510'.71'2—dc21   00-039649

Editor: Victoria Merecki
Production: Sonja Chapman
Cover design: Joseph DePinho, DePinho Graphic Design
Manufacturing: Louise Richardson

Printed in the United States of America on acid-free paper
    13 14 RRD 13 12 11

To Ann

(Continued from page iv)

Chapter 7 is an adaptation of Chapter 3 in *A Guide to K–12 Program Development in Mathematics,* copyright 1999 by the Connecticut State Board of Education. Adapted with permission.

Appendixes:

"It's Time to Abandon Computational Drudgery (But Not the Computation)" by Steven Leinwand is adapted from an article that originally appeared in *Education Week,* Volume 13, No. 20, February 19, 1994.

"Four Teacher-Friendly Postulates for Thriving in a Sea of Change" by Steven Leinwand originally appeared in *Mathematics Teacher,* September 1994. Reprinted with permission from *Mathematics Teacher,* copyright 1994 by the National Council of Teachers of Mathematics.

"Mathematics Program Leaders in Elementary, Middle, and High Schools" by Steven Leinwand is adapted from "Improving Student Achievement Through Designated District and School Mathematics Program Leaders," a position statement of the National Council of Supervisors of Mathematics. Reprinted with permission.

"Changing the System: Tidy Events and Messy Processes" by Steven Leinwand originally appeared as the "President's Message" in the *National Council of Supervisors of Mathematics Newsletter,* January 1997. Reprinted with permission.

"It's Still the Test, Stupid!" by Steven Leinwand originally appeared as the "President's Message" in the *National Council of Supervisors of Mathematics Newsletter,* March 1996. Reprinted with permission.

"Giving Students the Benefit of the Doubt" by Steven Leinwand originally appeared in *The Connecticut Mathematics Journal* of the Associated Teachers of Mathematics in Connecticut (ATOMIC), Spring 1995. Reprinted with permission.

"Beliefs: The Bedrock Upon Which Change is Built" by Steven Leinwand originally appeared in *The Connecticut Mathematics Journal* of the Associated Teachers of Mathematics in Connecticut (ATOMIC), Fall 1989. Reprinted with permission.

"Dreams, Ideas, and Tools for Making Middle School Mathematics Really Work: Thoughts for the New Standards Project" by Steven Leinwand reprinted with permission from *New Standards*™. The *New Standards*™ assessment system includes performance standards with performance descriptions, student work samples and commentaries, on-demand examinations, and a portfolio system. For more information contact the National Center on Education and the Economy, 202-783-3668 or <http:/www.ncee.org>.

Special thanks to Michael Linnetz and Charles H. Shoosham III for their contributions.

Contents

Introduction

Helping People Change

Changing people's behavior is one of the most difficult aspects of leadership. We know that people cannot do what they cannot envision. People will not do what they do not believe is possible. People will not support what they do not understand. And people will avoid those changes whose consequences are uncertain or feared. So it is with school mathematics as we enter the twenty-first century.

Students, teachers, and parents all need help and guidance to make the changes in curriculum, instruction, and assessment that are being called for in national standards for school mathematics. This help and guidance must come from school leaders—principals and other administrators—who help people envision the possible, show people what can be done, broaden people's understanding of why change is being made, and garner support for these changes within the broader community.

Providing this type of leadership is never easy. It is particularly difficult amid the public controversy that surrounds mathematics today. And it is particularly difficult without a set of understandings, perspectives, and tools that all effective leaders need at their disposal.

This book addresses the need for broader understanding, clearer perspective, and effective and easy-to-use tools by serving as a guidebook for mathematics improvement for school leaders. As a toolkit, this book provides principals and other school leaders with a broad array of strategies, a diverse arsenal of ammunition, and several "how-to" game plans for providing the leadership in kindergarten through twelfth grade mathematics. It is designed to provide reasonable and cogent answers to many of the questions that educators face when they are called upon to deal with a school or district's mathematics program. And it is written to help assure that all of America's mathematics classrooms better meet the higher expectations that result from changing societal and economic forces at work in every corner of our society and our economy.

In short, this book is written to help school leaders help the people they work with to change their beliefs and biases, their perspectives and understandings, and ultimately their behaviors—all in pursuit of higher levels of mathematics achievement by greater numbers of students.

Sensible
Mathematics

1 *Mediating, Forestalling, and Even Winning the Math Wars*

School principals and other school leaders face an enormous challenge when it comes to elementary, middle, and high school mathematics. The issues teachers face today in providing high-quality mathematics programs are not trivial. Resolving these issues in ways that best serve the young people in our schools is not easy. Balancing the often competing interests and positions of students, teachers, and parents in the face of single-minded pressures for higher test scores is difficult. And maintaining focus on what is best for students amid the tensions that abound when people are being asked to change is hard to do.

Although, for a long time, mathematics was the least controversial of school subjects, in recent years, it has become a raging battleground. Teachers and parents have become ensnared in disagreements over what to teach and even how to teach it. Confusion, emotion-laden arguments, and uncertainty surround discussions about what path to follow. Reformers are accused of "watering down" the curriculum, and proponents of the status quo are branded as "out of touch" with changes in society. In fact, just as educators have finally learned to resort to common sense and compromise to resolve long-simmering phonics versus whole language controversy, along comes what many are finding to be an even uglier and more intractable war over school mathematics.

Consider just a few of the troubling questions that principals and other school leaders are being asked to deal with:

- How much paper-and-pencil computation should be taught to best prepare students for a world in which calculators and computers do computation far more quickly and accurately?

- How do we transform mathematics programs that have traditionally sorted out the successful students from the unsuccessful ones with ruthless efficiency into programs that truly empower all students?

- How do we convince parents that the mathematics that "worked so well for me" is not the mathematics that best serves their children?
- How do we support teachers who, having been positively appraised and rewarded for using traditional "teaching by telling" approaches, now must shift instructional practices to meet higher and different expectations?

Enter the leader. Whether a principal, a curriculum director, a mathematics program supervisor, or other school leader, someone needs to have reasonable answers to these and other questions or, as has happened in many communities, mathematics reform efforts get undermined, sidetracked, or abandoned completely.

Some Background

In 1989, the National Council of Teachers of Mathematics (NCTM) launched the education standards movement and overturned the kindergarten to twelfth grade mathematics apple cart with the publication of *Curriculum and Evaluation Standards for School Mathematics*. After a decade of sporadic reform efforts and a crescendo of controversy, NCTM is now re-iterating and elaborating upon its core positions and visions for school mathematics with the publication of *Principles and Standards for School Mathematics*.

In a nutshell, the approximately 1,000 pages that comprise four volumes of standards* call for a mathematics curriculum more responsive to the needs of the twenty-first century than to the nineteenth century. These standards advocate a broader curriculum, adjusted in response to changing priorities, and changes in instructional practices, designed to meet the needs of a far greater portion of the student population. They call for a shift in emphasis from merely getting answers to exercises to finding and justifying solutions to problems. In addition, they recommend that mathematics be taught in ways that help students make sense of key ideas and concepts and in ways that promote communication, connections, and reasoning.

On the surface, this seems to be a reasonable agenda. Yet in classrooms across America, teachers and administrators are asking "Why bother?" "Why bother paying attention to these standards, both old and new?" "Why bother putting the time and effort into changing what I do,

---

Curriculum and Evaluation Standards for School Mathematics, 1989; *Professional Standards for Teaching*, 1991; *Assessment Standards*, 1995, and *Principles and Standards for School Mathematics*, 2000.

especially when it's so likely to be criticized and questioned?" "Why should I make changes that are almost certain to make my life harder?" The simple fact is that the changes being advocated *do* make people's lives harder. As educators, we are being asked to do more, to do things differently, and to be more productive—often with no more time, no more training, and no greater resources.

Once again, enter the leader. Principals and other school leaders must be able to confidently and knowledgeably respond and, when necessary, provide support and guidance. In the absence of cogent answers to these "why bother" questions and tangible support for those willing to take risks, little change will occur, frustration will mount, and students will suffer.

Common Situations

Consider just a few of the situations that arise when mathematics programs are being revised:

- Teachers, who are being asked to change, and parents, who are being asked to accept change, need to be convinced that there really is a need for change.

- People assume this round of change is just another fad, not unlike the "new math," and can be ignored, assured that "this too will soon pass."

- Teachers ask for assurance that there will be a long-term commitment to these changes.

- Parents want to be assured that their children are not being used as guinea pigs.

- Teachers and parents worry about the emphasis on "basics" in the new curriculum, fearful that their children will not learn what they believe is essential.

Again, these are situations that require informed leaders. Everywhere that improvements have been made and changes implemented, one will find one or more individuals who knew which battles to pick, who mediated conflicts, and who artfully kept the momentum moving and the pressure on. Someone took a potentially dangerous and destructive situation and prevented disaster. Someone stepped up and responded to the concerns. Someone stepped up and provided leadership.

Success Stories

Now consider just a few successful scenarios:

- After a year of piloting new instructional materials, a new and somewhat untraditional textbook program is selected. During the first two years of implementation, monthly professional development sessions are held, grade-level meetings are conducted, and teachers are given the opportunity to observe colleagues using these materials. Parents are informed about the programs during the pilot year and, once one is adopted, are given frequent updates about the implementation.

- Concerned about a history of significant and intractable achievement gaps between primarily white students on the one hand and primarily minority students on the other, the school board directs administrators to plan and implement a comprehensive initiative to narrow this gap. A blue-ribbon panel comprised of teachers, administrators, parents, and community leaders is created. Test scores are disaggregated and carefully analyzed in terms of skills and concepts to determine where gaps do and do not exist. Teachers from high- and low-achieving schools who volunteer are videotaped so that instructional practices can be studied and compared. Finally, a plan involving new forms of professional development, new instructional materials (including state-of-the-art software), and after-school and Saturday support programs is devised and implemented. Two years later, although not eliminated entirely, the gap is half as large and steadily narrowing.

- Reacting to a lack of improvement in state assessment results, a high school mathematics department recommends the adoption of a new integrated program that has been the source of great controversy in a neighboring community. Letters are sent to parents comparing the new program to the traditional program, honest representations are made about the stagnant test results and unimpressive SAT scores, and a public, teacher-led awareness evening is conducted for parents, the board of education, and the community at large.

In every case, a principal or other school leader makes the difference. He or she carefully analyzes the situation and strategically plans a course of action. In every case, teachers are active players, partnering with administrators, to ensure that the needs and potential concerns of diverse constituencies are addressed early in the change process. This book addresses specific strategies that school leaders can use to create their own success stories.

2 Making the Case for Change: Strategies and Compelling Examples

One of the responsibilities of leadership, at both the school and district levels, is building a case for change and then presenting this case to teachers and other colleagues, and to parents and other members of the community in a convincing and compelling manner. Effective leaders convey confidence in the changes they advocate. They make their support for these changes clear, and they assure others that careful thought has been given to these decisions.

In the case of reforming and improving school mathematics, principals and other school leaders must use the logic of a geometric proof and the powerful examples of effective debate to craft convincing arguments in support of doing things differently. People—particularly the vocal skeptics that we all encounter—need to be reassured that the changes being proposed are based on reason, experience, and best thinking, not on the basis of expediency or jumping on the latest bandwagon.

To make as compelling and convincing a case as possible, I have often used a four-part outline:

1. The world of work and the expectations of effective citizenship have changed dramatically—especially as they pertain to the ubiquitous reliance on technology to enhance productivity. It follows that the mathematics that students will need to thrive amidst these changes must change as well.

2. The expectations that society sets for schools and the needs that schools are required to meet are higher than ever before. It follows that more students need to master more mathematics than ever before.

3. Young people are different in important ways from their predecessors of just a few years ago. It follows that the methods used to teach these students must be different from the techniques used for previous generations.

5

4. There is ample evidence that, despite pockets of excellence and achievement, the traditional program fails to respond to these changing conditions and that mere tinkering at the edges will not produce the mathematical outcomes we need.

This chapter looks at each of these "domains of change" and outlines the process of building the case for the reform of school mathematics programs. Specific strategies for adapting the various components of this outline to one's own situation are presented at the end of each section.

Changes in Our Society

The World of Work

Because one of the primary purposes of all schooling is to prepare the next generation for productive placement in the workforce, it is reasonable to look at changes in workplace expectations for guidance on why and how to shift school mathematics. Some of the changes are obvious, others are less evident. Among the most obvious changes are those related to an increasingly high-tech workplace that requires more mathematical know-how than ever before to maintain productivity and economic competitiveness. It is critical, however, to recognize that what is required is *not* the mathematical know-how of increasingly obsolete skills like factoring trinomials or simplifying radicals. Instead, what is required are increasingly prevalent mathematical understandings like rates of change, statistics, and functions. Less and less are employees called upon to execute calculations with pencil and paper, but more and more are they expected and required to know when and why to perform a particular calculation.

Figure 2-1 captures one end of the continuum of what is required in today's world of work. The figure shows an adaptation of a familiar retail establishment's employment test and represents a clear example of entry-level mathematics requirements in today's world. The test prohibits calculators, but look at the balance among the items:

two extremely simple computation problems that no one should need a calculator for

two word problems that both involve making change

two essay problems that remind us once again of the role of thinking and reasoning

Employment tests like these are marvelous examples of the fact that some degree of computational skill is still important, but that the ability to solve problems and use thinking and reasoning to explain what you would do are equally important. It is reasonable to ask whether the bal-

---

Employment Test
(No Calculators Please)

1. 20.00
    − 5.79
    ——————

2. 3.59 + 4.88 + .79

3. If a customer's purchase came to $2.14 and she gave you a $10 bill, what change would you give her?

4. If the customer gave you a $10 bill, a $5 bill, and a quarter for a purchase that came to $11.21, what change would you give him?

5. What would you do if a customer complained that you gave him too little change?

6. What do you consider to be the two most important qualifications of a retail store employee?

Figure 2-1 Sample employment test for a retail business

ance found in this test is reflected by a relatively equivalent balance in one's mathematics curriculum.

If Figure 2-1 represents entry-level employment, a higher level of expectations, representing the other end of the continuum, can be found in the data generated daily by HMOs and other managed care operations. Surgeons in America today are monitored and evaluated closely on the basis of average cost per patient for such activities as the number of minutes in the operating room, cost of medical-surgical supplies, days in intensive care, etc. This close quantitative analysis of surgeons is but one example of the degree to which nearly all employees face a broad array of data upon which they are expected to make critical decisions. In the case of the HMO data on surgeons, the critical data analysis questions are: What recommendations would you make to each of these doctors on the basis of these data? How much confidence would you have in these recommendations? And what additional information would you like to have before making additional suggestions?

I often share examples like these with teachers and parents to help make the case that without significant changes, the traditional skill-based approach to mathematics fails to prepare students for either end of the employment spectrum. I often ask teachers and parents to think about their brothers and their sisters, their brothers-in-law and sisters-in-law, and other relatives and to consider the jobs these family members currently hold. I ask them to think about what mathematics is required in these positions and how they think the mathematics is done. I then share the following frequently referenced business and industry expectations for school mathematics (National Council of Teachers of Mathematics, [NCTM] 1989, p. 4) that have been attributed to Henry Pollak, the retired applied mathematician at Bell Labs:

Business and Industry Expectations for School Mathematics

- the ability to set up problems with the appropriate operations
- knowledge of a variety of techniques to approach and work on problems
- understanding of the underlying mathematical features of a problem
- the ability to work with others on problems
- the ability to see the applicability of mathematical ideas to common and complex problems
- preparation for messy problem situations because most real problems are not well formulated
- belief in the utility and value of mathematics

Finally, I ask teachers and parents to reflect on the gap between the traditional expectations of school mathematics programs on the one hand and the newer expectations cited in Pollak's list and in the jobs currently held by their relatives on the other.

> ***Strategy 2.1:***   *Use classroom investigations on "How mathematics is used in the world of work" to gather various artifacts like the employment test and HMO data previously presented. These materials—rarely limited to just rule-based skills and memorized procedures—serve as excellent ammunition for helping people understand why school mathematics programs must expand their focus on problem solving, communication, and conceptual understanding. A strategically placed "How our parents use mathematics" bulletin board can be a powerful tool for changing perceptions.*

The Impact of Technology

A second category of massive change is the impact of technology—in the form of calculators and computers—that has brought databases, spreadsheets, and the Internet to nearly every home and office and has supported an unprecedented increase in productivity. These changes from a paper-and-pencil world of ledger books to a calculator and computer world of millions of calculations per second cannot be ignored in the classrooms of America. This is particularly important because the technology has rendered some mathematics less important, other mathematics more important than ever, and still other mathematics finally accessible to all.

Just as calculators and computers have changed, if not eliminated, many jobs, they have also changed, if not eliminated, many elements of the mathematics curriculum and forced a reconsideration of how this mathematics curriculum is presented. Just as calculators and computers have made employees and businesses far more efficient and productive, they can also enhance the efficiency and productivity of teachers and schools. Just as it is inconceivable to run business or industry without cutting-edge technology, it is inconceivable to run schools that are expected to prepare students for the future unless all students have access to appropriate technology.

Computers and the Internet are rapidly changing nearly every aspect of our economic and social lives. They are the means by which we communicate, coordinate, and conduct commerce, and they are the engines of massive change. They enhance human capability in nearly every field of endeavor. To believe that students can be kept from these tools is to live in a dream world. To believe that technology won't eventually have as great an impact on schools as it does elsewhere is to ignore the sweep of history.

When our washing machine breaks down, we turn to an equivalent piece of technology at the laundromat or we wait for our own to be repaired. We no longer resort to the washboard technology that we neither have access to nor know how to use. Similarly, when a calculator is lost or loses battery power, we borrow a replacement, replace the battery, or

> **Strategy 2.2:**   *As part of a data-gathering exercise, ask students to interview their parents and gather information on what tools—one's brain, pencil and paper, a calculator, or a computer—are used to perform mathematics on the job and at home. Students can generate lists of when their parents are most likely to do mathematics mentally or rely only on estimates, when pencil and paper are still used, and when a calculator or computer is the preferred tool. The graphs and student reports make excellent fodder for presentations and discussions with parents about changes in a school's mathematics program.*

simply buy a new one. We rarely resort to the paper-and-pencil technology that is either too time-consuming or that we no longer remember how to do. It is interesting to note that when the power goes out, for better or worse, the world shuts down. The fact that the power can go out in most of America's schools and education marches on is strong testimony to how little reliance is made of what most consider the enabling variable for change.

Effective Citizenship

Thirdly, there are the demands of effective citizenship—exemplified by such controversial issues as tax policy, solid waste disposal, open space versus the development of suburban sprawl, integrating schools, and reducing crime. To respond intelligently to these and similar issues as well as to assure a truly informed electorate, citizens need an unprecedented degree of mathematical literacy. Jim Rubillo,* a professor at Bucks County Community College in Pennsylvania, has generated a list of "Life's Key Questions." The list includes:

- What are the chances?
- What are the risks?
- Are the figures accurate?
- How fast is the situation changing?
- Can things get better or worse?

Each of these, and many more, requires a deeper and broader understanding of mathematics than ever before.

Accordingly, no matter what one's position on changing the mathematics curriculum, it is impossible and irresponsible to ignore the fact that daily we are

- bombarded with data that must be organized and analyzed to make decisions;
- surrounded by change that must be mathematized to be understood and from which predictions can be made;
- forced to deal with ambiguity and uncertainly that exist in most situations and that can be quantified with mathematics; and
- confronted in countless situations with a dazzling array of patterns from which we try to make generalizations and draw conclusions.

_____

*Presentation handout, "Why Study Math," James Rubillo, available at www.scopethescene.com/JimRubillo/whymath3.htm.

Figure 2-2 Changes in church attendance and Bible reading, 1991 and 1998

In case there is any doubt, just look at these selected pieces found during a casual perusal of *USA Today* for May 27, 1998:

- In the "USA Snapshots: A look at statistics that shape the nation" there is a graph showing changes in church attendance and Bible reading (see Figure 2-2).

- In one article, Joe Garagiola takes aim at snuff tobacco and provides statistics on teenager's use of tobacco (see Figure 2-3).

- A full-page ad for a portable computer includes the specifications shown in Figure 2-4.

- An editorial titled "Loopholes Let Wealthy Seniors Access Medicaid Funds" provide statistics on Medicaid's "bleak" future (see Figure 2-5).

Teens' tobacco choices

Percent of high school students who said they used tobacco products at least once a month (1997 figures):

	Total	Male	Female
Cigarettes	36.4%	37.7%	34.7%
Smokeless	9.3%	15.8%	1.5%
Cigars	22.0%	31.2%	10.8%

Source: U.S. Centers for Disease Control and Prevention

Figure 2-3 What do teenagers smoke?

The Affordable Portable

12.1″ SVGA DSTN Color Display

16 MB SDRAM (expandable to 192 MB)

2 MB Graphics Accelerator w/64K colors

Modular 8X min/20K max CD-ROM Drive

Modular 3.5″ Diskette Drive

2 GB Ultra ATA Hard Drive

$1699 as low as $59/month

Figure 2-4 Specifications for a portable computer

- An article titled: "Cholesterol Pill May Help the Healthy" states:

  After five years, the treated group had 25% lower LDL levels and was 37% less likely to have suffered a heart attack, unstable angina or sudden cardiac death. But the actual numbers of such events was quite low in both groups. Five years of lovastatin treatment in 1,000 patients would prevent 12 heart attacks, seven cases of unstable angina and 17 bypass or angioplasty procedures, the researchers write.

What more compelling evidence of how ubiquitous mathematics has become in our society could one ask for? And what more compelling ev-

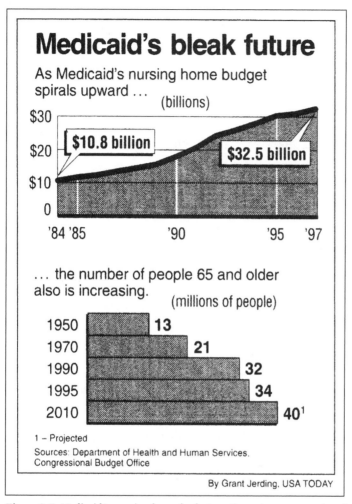

Figure 2-5 *Medicaid's nursing home budget continues to grow—as does the number of people over 65*

idence of the gap between real-world mathematics and traditional school mathematics could one find? Look at the mathematical understanding expected of average citizens trying to make informed and wise decisions for themselves and their families:

- Does this array of data make sense? Is any of it intuitively questionable or likely to be wrong?

- How could a minister incorporate the information in the graph on "Spiritual revival?" into next Sunday's sermon?

- What important conclusions can be drawn from the graph on "Teen's Smoking Choices"? What policies should Congress adopt in light of these figures?
- Is the advertised computer a good buy? How does it compare to comparable portable computers?
- Is the Medicaid problem really one of wealthy seniors or, on the basis of the graphs, is the entire system doomed? What are reasonable projections for 2000, 2005, and 2010? What additional data would be helpful?
- What additional information would you want before signing up to take lovastatin to lower cholesterol levels?

What clearer evidence could there be that we live in a world of data, a world of change, and a world of ambiguity? And what clearer evidence could there be that the paper-and-pencil, drill-and-practice, memorize-and-regurgitate practices of the traditional mathematics curriculum ill prepare young people to deal with important questions like those listed here?

In short, more than ever, mathematics is everywhere. It is the language of data, the language of change, and the language of patterns. It is the tool that helps to quantify situations and the language that helps us make sense of phenomena. It is the gut conceptual understanding of the magnitude of numbers, of a sense of what is likely or unlikely, of what is reasonable or unreasonable, and of what's changing and how fast. It is *not* a set of memorized procedures that are now almost universally done by machine, nor an array of trivial-pursuit-like formulas that are rarely retained ten minutes after the last exam. It is this increasingly ubiquitous nature of mathematics, in conjunction with its longstanding practicality, that makes change in what we teach and how we teach and assess it so imperative.

> **Strategy 2.3:** *As seen in the* USA Today *example, the newspaper is often a cornucopia of data and other examples of how mathematics arises daily in the real world. An interesting experiment to conduct (or to challenge others to conduct) is to compare the percentage of time or pages allocated to specific mathematical topics in the traditional curriculum with the percentage of times these same mathematical topics are found in the news, business, sports, and entertainment pages of the local newspaper. People are often astounded at how poor a match one often finds.*

Hopefully, these examples and suggested strategies help people reach the conclusion that the requirements of productive work, the impact of technology, and the demands of effective citizenship provide a strong basis for commensurate changes in what mathematics must be valued and taught to students who will live most of their lives in the twenty-first century.

Changes in Expectations

Perhaps even more important than better meeting the needs of a changing workplace and society is the increasing necessity for mathematics to meet the needs of a much greater percentage of students than has ever before been the case.

It used to be so easy. Teachers lectured and students listened. Teachers showed students how to get answers and students then practiced the procedures. Homework and tests were based largely on memorization of these procedures and applications came last, if at all. Some learned, many failed. Some enjoyed this ritual, many still suffer from its scars. But most importantly, the system ensured that the smart got smarter, the average stayed average, and the weakest never caught on or up. For most of the 1950s, '60s, and even '70s this arrangement worked. Schools did a magnificent job of meeting society's needs for a few mathematically gifted citizens, a few more mathematically able, and most with only limited mathematical understanding. Just look at how the mathematics curriculum has been used to sort students into "winners" and "losers":

- Second graders are often expected to master subtraction with regrouping using only symbols, despite their limited mastery of prerequisite understandings of place value or addition and subtraction facts—leading many to a premature self-concept of being mathematically inept.

- Paper-and-pencil proficiency with fractions continues to be a prerequisite for the study of algebra, despite the fact that most key algebraic ideas require little or no skill with fractions.

- The critical study of functions, statistics, and trigonometry are too often denied to students unable to master the arithmetic of polynomials or the simplification of rational expressions, despite the fact that the former requires very little of the latter.

- Pre-med students are required to pass calculus, despite the fact that derivatives and integrals have almost nothing to do with the effective practice of medicine.

In each of these cases, the mathematics curriculum has erected gates that have effectively kept many from moving on. We have implemented a curriculum that has systematically undermined both teachers and students, guaranteeing that only a few will succeed. And it bears repeating: for many years, this arrangement worked for schools, worked for society, and resulted in nearly none of the concerns or criticisms so widespread today.

Another way that the interaction between students and school mathematics plays out is captured in a most compelling fashion in *Everybody Counts:*

> Virtually all young children like mathematics. They do mathematics naturally, discovering patterns and making conjectures based on observation. Natural curiosity is a powerful teacher, especially for mathematics. Unfortunately, as children become socialized by school and society, they begin to view mathematics as a rigid system of externally dictated rules governed by standards of accuracy, speed, and memory. Their view of mathematics shifts gradually from enthusiasm to apprehension, from confidence to fear. Eventually, most students leave mathematics under duress, convinced that only geniuses can learn it. Later, as parents, they pass this conviction on to their children. Some even become teachers and convey this attitude to their students. (National Research Council [NRC], 1989, pp. 43–44)

But just as the need for universal reading literacy forced schools to adopt new curricula and new instructional techniques so as to expand the proportion of students leaving schools as successful readers, so too must schools now adopt similar changes in mathematics to reach new levels of mathematical literacy.

> ***Strategy 2.4:*** *Conduct a discussion at a faculty meeting or a mathematics department meeting on ways in which students are sorted in our school and ways in which the opportunities students have are limited by our policies and practices—often created with the best of intentions. List these policies and practices, the obstacles (both overt and covert) that have been erected, and discuss the implications of changing these practices or removing some of these obstacles. (For example, the practice of using reading scores as a criterion for entry into eighth grade algebra has a long history and interesting implications. Similarly, the practice of pulling weaker students out of mainstream mathematics instruction for supplemental—and other less rigorous—instruction clearly communicates different expectations.)*

Changes in Students

An often forgotten—or conveniently ignored—piece of the puzzle is the students themselves and the enormous changes in the experiences and attitudes with which they arrive in school. Today's student

- has been weaned on fast-paced Nintendo, Sega, and Sony Playstation video games;
- has come of age to the beat of MTV, the blare of boom boxes, and the pulsating rap of hip-hop; and
- thrives in the wired world of the computer, the Internet, and e-mail.

It's no secret to any classroom teacher that the days of a well-mannered class sitting quietly and obediently in rows, completing column after column of exercises are long gone. But rather than dream wistfully for these "good old days," it is necessary to compare the fast-paced, highly visual world of today's students with the equally fast-paced, computer-driven world of commerce with its faxes, e-mails, pagers, and FedExes.

To bolster this argument, consider some of today's reality:

- American youth spend much more time per year in front of electronic screens in their homes—TV, computers, and video games—than they spend in school.
- In homes with children, subscriptions to the Internet are nearly as common as subscriptions to newspapers.
- More than 70 percent of teenagers said they would give up TV before giving up their computer or the Internet.
- Cable TV took twenty-five years to get to ten million subscribers. The VCR took nine years. The World Wide Web only five years!

In the face of cultural changes of this magnitude, it is impossible to believe that school mathematics can be immune to change as well. But sometimes the case is best made closer to home, where I frequently find my rather typical teenager at his computer juggling several Internet sites from which he is downloading material for a social studies paper he is writing, two instant messages from friends, and a slew of e-mails to which he is in the process of responding. I am often struck by how similar his fast-paced electronic world is to the offices and businesses I frequent, and how different it is from most schools and classrooms. Is it any wonder that he and so many others are so bored in school? Isn't it amazing that one of the most common concerns at focus groups on textbook design is how "busy" the pages look? Isn't it time to recognize and address the growing gap between our students' real lives and their lives in school? Isn't it time to narrow the gap between the realities of the world of work and the realities of the typical mathematics program?

Thus, not only do the critics of reform conveniently ignore how much the world has changed, more dangerously, they fail to acknowledge how much our children have changed. In clinging to the traditions of the past and ignoring the impact of computers, fast-paced video games, the Internet, and the incessant beat of MTV, rap, and hip-hop, the skeptics condemn the next generation to mathematics instruction too often unrelenting in its boredom, astounding in its irrelevance, and frightening in its ability to demean and demoralize!

> *Strategy 2.5:*   *Because many people, including parents and teachers, are often surprisingly oblivious to the magnitude of change in students themselves, it is often useful to gather data as part of mathematics instruction that can also be used to better inform people about today's students. Teachers can be encouraged to share survey data that students collect and summarize on such topics as*
>
> - *the interests of students in our class versus the topics found in our math book;*
>
> - *the number of calculators and computers found in my home and how they are used;*
>
> - *five things I enjoy doing and why; five things I don't enjoy doing and why.*
>
> *Such data makes powerful fodder in principal's newsletters, school bulletin boards, and at parent meetings. In the world of business, this data is comparable to "knowing one's customers." It can be used to better meet the needs of these customers as well as provide a rationale for those changes that are required to better meet these needs.*

Once again, the evidence is clear. As expectations have been raised and as students have changed in significant ways, one must face the obvious conclusion that the mathematics we teach and the manner in which we teach it must undergo commensurate changes to respond appropriately. Chapter 3 begins to describe these changes in detail.

What the Traditional Program Hath Wrought

This next task of debunking the so-called accomplishments of the traditional program is perhaps the most difficult, but perhaps the most important, part of making a case for change. After all, there are pockets of success, even excellence, within all schools and districts. In addition, we have all spent so much time putting the best spin on even mediocre results that suggesting that all is not well can be a daunting task. However, many parents and skeptics assume that an easy solution is merely continuing to do all that we have been doing and just add on a little more that is new. Such a compromise approach ignores the fact that some of what we have been doing is no longer needed and some has never really worked well at all.

One way to make the point that there really were no "good old days" and that the traditional program has a long history of failure is to collect anecdotal tidbits that reveal the seriousness of the mathematics achievement problem. Several of my favorite examples follow.

Once again, our daily newspapers often provide the best insight into just how serious the problem is, as is seen in this snippet from the *San Jose Mercury News:*

> And some food companies have started rewriting recipes after calls from customers who fail to grasp that a 9×13 baking pan is the same as a 13×9 pan. And that egg whites are not egg shells.

It's fairly obvious what happens when measurement topics are subordinated to mindless computational procedures or when the measurement chapter is skipped entirely. So we must recognize the consequences of making the mistake of maintaining a curriculum that has never produced widespread mathematical literacy.

In addition to the myth of some glorious return to some never existing past, there is the daily confrontation with how society's need for mathematical know-how is seriously outpacing the extant quantity of such know-how. One does not have to look far for examples of how number sense, measurement, and statistical deficiencies come home to roost. Consider the shamefully common events described on the front page of the January 25, 1995 *Waterbury* (CT) *American*, which featured a photograph of a large tractor-trailer stuck under an overpass. Under the headline "Faulty Bridge Sign Traps Truck" one reads:

> When city workers measured a bridge over West Main Street last fall, their efforts fell a little short—10 inches short to be exact. After yet another tractor-trailer got wedged beneath the railroad bridge near Sperry Street, Traffic Department workers decided to re-measure the clearance Wednesday morning. To their surprise, the clearance is 10 inches shorter than the 13 feet, 8 inches noted on the warning sign before the bridge.
>
> The clearance is 12 feet 10 inches. Sgt. John Hyland, the city's traffic engineer, said employees of the paint and sign division measured the bridge in September or October, and that the new signs were installed January 18 to replace the old ones. He said the person or people who made the mistake will face disciplinary action.
>
> Saturday night, an 18-wheeler driven by John E. Thomas, 35, of Waterbury got stuck beneath the bridge. He was able to drive the truck, measuring 13 feet, 6 inches in height, back to the Sorensen Transportation Co. in Bethany. Thomas, who was hired by the company in November, said he was terminated from his job Monday because the accident happened during his 3-month probation.

All because of one silly measurement error!

For anyone not yet convinced that there is an achievement problem in mathematics that rears its ugly head in more and more inconvenient and even dangerous ways, consider:

- how frustrating it is when your car is "repaired" by a high school dropout who used to tune an engine with merely an ear and a wrench and who now must rely on digital readout to accurately tune today's high-tolerance and highly finicky engines; or

- how scary it is that the overnight maintenance on the commercial jet's engines might have been completed by someone with less than a full understanding of the difference between 0.1 and 0.01; or

- how deadly it can be when hospital ICUs are staffed with people whose understanding of the metric system and of proportions can lead to serious errors in calculating drug doses and IV drip rates.

And then, there's the following letter I received in the mail.

Dear Steve:

I am an attorney. About ten years ago, I was working for a small firm in Connecticut when my boss assigned me a case involving the defense of a drunk driver. The defendant had been arrested after a routine traffic stop (there had been no accident). After checking the vehicle's registration, the defendant was given the field sobriety tests. After failing the walk-a-straight-line and touch-your-nose tests, he was given a breath test which registered 0.13 (0.10 being the legal limit). At the police station, he consented to a blood test which registered 0.15.

Here are the facts:

1. Connecticut's drunk driving law requires that the operator exceed the legal limit while operating his or her motor vehicle.
2. Twenty minutes after last operating a motor vehicle, the defendant had a blood alcohol level of .13, and sixty minutes after last operating a motor vehicle, his level was .15.
3. Therefore, his level was increasing and there is no way to be sure that he was above .10 when he was operating the motor vehicle.

His case was dismissed!

Obviously, there is a basic flaw in my argument—both .13 and .15 are squarely within the standard deviations of both tests. In fact, from a purely statistical analysis, the tests were consistent and proved beyond a reasonable doubt that my client was drunk.

Interestingly enough, the prosecutor missed the flaw, but the judge did not. Why the dismissal, then? The judge told me: "I know that your argument is faulty, but I also know that the prosecution will never in a million years be able to convince a jury of that fact. No jury will understand the numbers, and therefore, no jury would convict your client."

The bottom line here is that a drunk driver slipped through the cracks and is free to drive a car because of rampant mathematical illiteracy!

Just think how easy it should be for the prosecutors of the world to turn to a flip chart before the jury and pencil in the data:

20 minutes—.13 blood alcohol content

60 minutes—.15 blood alcohol content

And then, with a knowing and dignified flourish, the prosecutor sketches a vertical and horizontal axis. What a wonderful picture can be conjured up of "mathematics-to-the-rescue" (see Figure 2-6)—as the prosecutor plots (20, .13) and (60, .15) and connects then with a line that clearly passes above .10 on the vertical Blood Alcohol Content axis!

But alas, when jury members have been deprived of the opportunity to study algebra or when jury members' primary algebraic experiences entailed the mindless simplification of radicals and rational expressions, instead of a healthy dose of data analysis, there is little hope for conviction of the guilty.

> **Strategy 2.6:** *In addition to using examples like the ones recounted here or similar examples drawn from local media, principals and other school leaders can often find powerful ammunition in school and district*

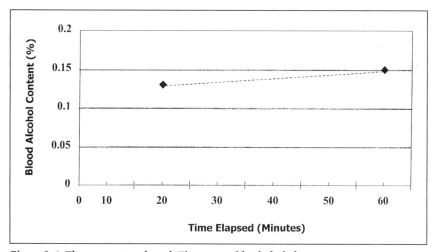

Figure 2-6 The prosecutor rebuttal: Time versus blood alcohol content

results on released test items. It is quite common to find reasonably high scores on relatively low-level types of test items entailing merely recall of vocabulary and memorized procedures. However, sharing relatively higher level test items—with usually much lower scores—can help rally both understanding and support for a more balanced curriculum.

Summing Up

By now the logic should be irrefutable: the world has changed dramatically. Because schools are expected to prepare young people for the world they will face, what we do in schools to prepare students for this changing world must change as well. Unfortunately, this role of preparing students for the future runs in direct conflict with the traditional role of schools to perpetuate the rich mores, lore, and traditions of our culture. And here is where the trouble begins. We find people equating the place of say the Civil War in the curriculum with say the place of long division. Both represent important traditions of our culture. However, one (obviously, the Civil War) is as interesting and as important today as it was yesterday, whereas the other (obviously, long division), is increasingly obsolete and serves no useful purpose in meeting the future needs students will face. To build an effective case for change, principals and other school leaders must use the magnitude of change in society at large as ammunition to address the implications of these changes on the mathematics curriculum and support commensurate changes in mathematics programs.

3 Responding to Changing Conditions: What to Expect and Advocate

Ideally, the ideas and strategies delineated in the previous chapter set the stage for change. Hopefully, they create a school, district, and community environment in which there is little disagreement that

- the magnitude of the changes in the world of work are large;
- mathematical literacy is a more important intellectual commodity than ever before;
- expectations have had to rise to keep pace;
- students and their motivations have changed significantly as well; and
- traditional approaches are unlikely to satisfy these changing conditions.

Now it's time for the heavy lifting. Given all of these changes, it should follow naturally that the mathematics curriculum must shift, instructional practices must be adjusted, and methods of assessing understanding must be altered. More specifically, NCTM and others are advocating:

- a shift in curriculum toward a deeper study of mathematical ideas and concepts and their uses in today's world;
- a shift in learning toward more active student involvement with mathematics;
- a shift in teaching toward classrooms as stimulating learning environments in which all students are given the opportunity to reach their mathematical potential; and
- a shift in assessment practices toward student evaluation that is based on many sources of evidence.

It's one thing to call for shifts. It's quite another to implement them. To begin this process, it is important that principals and other school leaders understand clearly what each of these shifts entails and what each would look like in classrooms. Only then can one articulately argue for such changes. What follows are encapsulated descriptions and examples of each of these shifts.

Curricular Shifts

In an abbreviated form, the heart of the revision to the K–12 mathematics curriculum stems from a clarion call for a "shift in emphasis from a curriculum dominated by an emphasis on memorization of isolated facts and procedures, and proficiency with paper and pencil skills, to one which emphasizes conceptual understandings, multiple representations and connections, mathematical modeling and mathematical problem solving" (NCTM, 1989, p. 125).

More specifically, at the K–8 level, this means a curriculum that emphasizes the applications of adding, subtracting, multiplying, and dividing whole numbers, decimals, and fractions in the contexts of buying and selling, comparing, measuring, predicting, and interpreting. Similarly, at the 9–12 level, this means a curriculum that replaces an emphasis on rules and procedures for manipulating symbols with an emphasis on using and applying mathematical concepts to formulate and solve a broad range of problems that arise in diverse situations entailing quantity, data, change, patterns, optimizing, scaling, measuring, predicting, and proving.

Figure 3-1 depicts this curricular shift as moving from a focus on procedures to a focus on creating and using mathematical models—that is, for example, from a focus on merely *how* to divide whole numbers to a focus on *when* and *why* to use of the operation of division. It attempts to convey the changing focus from procedures that are memorized to models that are understood and chosen. This figure also tries to clarify the ongoing interplay among grounding mathematics in the real world (situations and phenomena), mathematical symbols and language (mathematical representations), and finally solutions. In a world without calculators and computers, it makes sense for mathematics to focus primarily on the bottom half of the diagram, that is, the use of well-practiced and memorized procedures to convert mathematical representations to answers. However, in a world where calculators and computers do most procedural mathematics, we must shift our curricular focus to the top half of the diagram, that is, the use of mathematical models to convert diverse situations and phenomena into appropriate mathematical representations.

In the classroom, some of the implications of this shift are captured in Figures 3-2 and 3-3. One shows the shift from long division to using division to solve interesting problems. The other shows the shift from an algebra course driven by manipulating symbols to one driven by solving problems that develop algebraic thinking.

SITUATIONS AND PHENOMENA
(such as the lottery, gravity, interest, queuing, or trajectories)

are converted using appropriate

MATHEMATICAL MODELS
(such as multiplication, exponentiation, proportion, or linear function)

into

MATHEMATICAL REPRESENTATIONS
(such as an expression, an equation, a graph, a diagram, or a table)

which in turn are converted using appropriate

MATHEMATICAL PROCEDURES
(such a long division, squaring, factoring, solving, or proving)

into

SOLUTIONS
(such as answers, explanations, justifications, or proofs)

Figure 3-1 Shifting the curriculum

Where We've Been

Using only pencil and paper, find the quotient: $1.59 \div 10$

Where We're Moving To

Given the data: Big Macs cost $1.59 each and you have $10.00

With calculators available, consider and answer the following questions. In each case, show your work and explain how you arrived at your answer.

- Can you afford to buy 10? Why or why not?
- How many can you afford to buy? Did you remember to include tax?
- At what sales tax rate can you afford one additional Big Mac?
- Explain how you arrived at your answer.
- Create two additional questions that arise from this situation and this data.

Figure 3-2 Long division: Then and now

Where We've Been

Algebra has been a course for only some students that marched through a series of units like:

- variables and expressions
- signed numbers
- equations
- polynomials and exponents
- factoring
- fractions and rational expressions
- proportions and variation
- linear functions
- systems of equations
- quadratic equations

Algebra was tested with test items that asked students to:

- simplify
- solve
- factor
- graph

Where We're Moving To

Algebra should be a course for all students that includes a series of units like:

- the language of algebra: variables, expressions, integers
- data and the graphics calculator
- equations and problems: given the independent variable, what is the dependent variable and vice versa
- proportions, percents, and variation
- linear functions
- systems of equations and matrices
- exponential functions

Algebra should be tested with test items that ask students to:

- find
- express
- display
- represent
- demonstrate
- model
- solve

Figure 3-3 Algebra: Then and now

In both cases, the essence of this curricular shift is captured in the overarching objective of K–8 mathematics—then and now—presented in Figure 3-4.

One of the examples I use to help crystallize the need for this shift is the following excerpt from an article on dealing with jet lag that I stumbled upon several years ago in the *USAir Magazine:*

> Synchronizing the internal clock to local time generally takes from one to one and a half days per time zone (though for some people it can take twice as long.) For example, Tokyo is 14 time zones removed from New York, so it will take the average person nine days to adjust ($14 \div 1.5 = 9$).

Imagine my surprise when I wrestled with the discrepancy between my estimate of fourteen to twenty-one days (one to one and a half days for each of fourteen times zones) and the nine days asserted in the article. And how dare a reader question the supporting equation that apparently justifies the answer of nine days! But what better evidence can one find to help make the case that we have a serious mathematics achievement problem? The excerpt reminds us vividly that we have taught the average and below-average students *how* to divide (14 divided by 1.5 is indeed 9), but we have not taught enough students the far more important skills of deciding *when* and *why* to divide. Taken even further, the excerpt reminds us that we have taught most students how to get *answers to exercises* in preparation for a world that increasingly requires people to arrive at *solutions to problems.*

The Baby and the Bath Water Strategy

One approach that teachers and administrators can use to help make these difficult curriculum decisions is to systematically examine what is

---

Overarching K–8 mathematics curriculum objective THEN

Given a numerical computation problem, students will use pencil and paper and the appropriate algorithm to find the sum, difference, product, or quotient.

Overarching K–8 mathematics curriculum objective NOW

Given a problem situation with realistic data, students will decide whether to use the addition, subtraction, multiplication, or division key on a calculator and explain why that key will help determine a useful, quantitative result for the given problem.

Figure 3-4 K–8 curricular objectives: Then and now

still important to know and what is no longer important. We are often reminded not to "throw out the baby with the bath water." Less frequently are we reminded that what was once recognized as "baby" may now increasingly be "bath water." Therefore, one way to better grasp the changes described in this chapter is to see reform as an ongoing analysis of what components of the mathematics curriculum are still fully part of the "baby" and which components of the curriculum are either clearly or increasing part of the "bath water" that is best thrown away.

Here's a way to start these discussions. Despite claims of critics to the contrary, a mastery of one-digit number facts has always been and continues to be a critical part of the "baby." No set of standards and no framework from California to Connecticut has suggested abandoning mastery of number facts. Given that these facts (e.g., $17 - 8 = 9$, $7 \times 4 = 28$) are indispensable for estimation and for mental computation, and given that these facts are essential for a solid, confident number sense, it is inconceivable—even in a world of calculators—that they would be cast aside with the "bath water." In fact, mastery of number facts is more important than ever. But, if, for the first time in our history, *all* students are going to masterery these facts, we must expand our teaching repertoire beyond memorization and practice. Facts must be approached in contexts (e.g., simple price lists), with materials (e.g., counters, number lines, even fingers), via fact families (e.g., $4 \times 7 = 28$, $7 \times 4 = 28$, $28 \div 4 = 7$, and $28 \div 7, = 4$, to reduce memory load), and with attention to strategies ($8 + 9 = 17$ because $8 + 9$ is the same as $8 + 8$ or 16 plus 1 or the same as $8 + 10$ or 18 minus 1).

On the other side of the fence is multidigit paper-and-pencil computation. Given all of the changes previously discussed and the needs to expand the scope of the curriculum, it is time that multiplication and division with factors and divisors containing three or more digits, and computation with fractions, and mixed numbers with denominators like 7, 9, 11, or 13, finally be relegated as "bath water." Just as we have survived the elimination of the square root algorithm from the curriculum—but increased the emphasis on the concept of square root and where it is used—we can and will survive the elimination of complex, multidigit computation.

One effective method for helping to make these "baby versus bath water" decisions is to ask the question: Is this something that I want my own child to be able to do? When I realized that I was far more aghast that my twelve-year-old couldn't estimate the difference between $7\frac{1}{5}$ and $4\frac{6}{7}$ (with a practical answer of a little more than 2) rather than actually calculate the difference (a precise, but absurd $2\frac{12}{35}$), I began to clarify where the "baby–bath water" line was.

So at its core, this array of necessary shifts comes down to what we value. I am increasingly clear on what I value and present these values in the following list. It is the role of principals and other school leaders to clarify and publicize what they believe and use these beliefs to make and defend their decisions about mathematics curriculum, instruction, and assessment.

What Is Valued Now and in the Future

- Right answers
- Computational capability
- Knowledge of vocabulary
- Ability to solve word problems
- Ability to make reasonable estimates
- Ability to explain one's reasoning
- Ability to actually measure, construct, devise, display
- Ability to defend decisions and positions
- Ability to solve nonroutine problems
- Ability to formulate and solve your own problems

Instructional Shifts

The curricular shifts just discussed must be supported by changes in instructional approaches as well. Once again, *Everybody Counts* says it most compellingly:

> Evidence from many sources shows that the least effective mode for mathematics learning is the one that prevails in most of America's classrooms: lecturing and listening. Despite daily homework, for most students and most teachers, mathematics continues to be primarily a passive activity: teachers prescribe, students transcribe. Students simply do not retain for long what they learn by imitation from lectures, worksheets or routine homework. Presentation and repetition help students do well on standardized tests and lower-order skills, but they are generally ineffective as teaching strategies for long-term learning, for higher-order thinking, and for versatile problem solving. (NRC, 1989, p. 57)

Instead, our vision for mathematics instruction, supported by both research and the wisdom of practice, involves classrooms where students are regularly engaged in sustained work, inquiring about and working to make sense of mathematical ideas, and constructing personal meaning of these ideas.

For example, instead of merely posing the problem: 92 – 37 = ? and expecting that students will proceed in step-by-step fashion to regroup the

92 into 8 tens and 12 ones in order to "correctly" find the difference, the instructional shift that is essential would entail much of what is shown in Figure 3-5. Notice that this instruction includes, but goes well beyond, getting a correct answer, and focuses additionally on problem solving, the meaning of subtraction, estimation, and most importantly, alternative approaches to arriving at estimates and answers.

The Third International Mathematics and Science Study (TIMSS) videotaped study of classes in the United States, Germany, and Japan reinforces these instructional shifts by describing the steps in typical eighth grade mathematics lessons in these countries. Figure 3-6 summarized the differences in the common lesson scripts found in these countries and suggests serious consideration of what is typically found in Japanese classrooms that consistently produce higher levels of students achievement than American classrooms.

Another way of capturing the essence of the instructional shifts that are needed in mathematics can be extracted from the far less controversial world of the reading curriculum. It is widely accepted that effective reading instruction and assessment builds from literal comprehension to inferential comprehension to evaluative comprehension. There is widespread understanding that in order to be deemed powerful readers, all students must be exposed to and must master all three types of comprehension. In contrast, much of mathematics instruction begins and ends with literal comprehension, that is, the mathematical equivalent of "Who went to the store with Bobby?" Effective mathematics instruction must be expanded to include inferential comprehension and evaluative comprehension like that embodied in the questions in Figure 3-7.

Given: 92 − 37 = ?

Teachers might ask

1. Write a word problem, with realistic data, that would require someone to find this difference.

2. For the different problems that students read:

   - What is a reasonable estimate for your problem?
   - How did you get your estimate?
   - What is the actual answer to your problem?
   - Explain how you arrived at your answer.

Figure 3-5 Shifting instruction

The emphasis on understanding is evident in the steps typical of Japanese eighth grade mathematics lessons:

- Teacher poses a complex thought-provoking problem.
- Students struggle with the problem.
- Various students present ideas or solutions to the class.
- Class discusses the various solution methods.
- The teacher summarizes the class' conclusions.
- Students practice similar problems.

In contrast, the emphasis on skill acquisition is evident in the steps common to most U.S. and German math lessons:

- Teacher instructs students in a concept or skill.
- Teacher solves example problems with class.
- Students practice on their own while the teacher assists individual students.

Source: Third International Mathematics and Science Study; unpublished tabulations, Videotape Classroom Study, UCLA, 1996.

Figure 3-6 Comparison of the steps typical of eighth grade mathematics lessons in Japan, the U.S., and Germany

The progression of questioning in good instruction can be captured very simply. When pencils cost 3¢ each and pens cost 4¢ each, the following set of questions and answers demonstrates an instructional shift that goes beyond just a correct answer. Note how instead of stopping at the correct answer, the teacher pushes instruction to higher-order questions that focus on the student's broader understanding and ability to explain.

TEACHER: How much will it cost to purchase one pencil and one pen?

STUDENT: 7¢

TEACHER: Good, how did you get 7¢?

STUDENT: I added.

TEACHER: Great. Why did you add?

STUDENT: Because I needed both items and you add when you put things together.

Literal comprehension:	What is the answer? What is the question asking you to find?
Inferential comprehension:	Why do you think Amanda did that? Why do you think the author made that suggestion?
Evaluative comprehension:	Is Sam's answer reasonable? Why or why not? What good is it to know that?

Figure 3-7 Reading and mathematics comprehension parallels

The instructional shifts described here can all be categorized as methods of fostering a thinking and reasoning curriculum: that is, a curriculum that values correct answers, not as an end unto themselves, but as a means to do and learn so much more.

NCTM's *Professional Standards for Teaching Mathematics* reiterates these points when it advocates mathematics teaching that empowers all students by shifting toward:

- classrooms as mathematical communities—away from classrooms as simply a collection of individuals;

- logic and mathematical evidence as verification—away from the teacher as the sole authority for right answers;

- mathematical reasoning—away from merely memorizing procedures;

- conjecturing, inventing, and problem solving—away from an emphasis on mechanistic answer-finding; and

- connecting mathematics, its ideas, and its applications—away from treating mathematics as a body of isolated concepts and procedures.

The "Let's Go to the Videotape" Strategy

One approach that teachers and administrators can use to help examine and shift instructional practices is to videotape and collegially discuss selected lessons. Many schools have begun an examination of teaching practices with the six lessons found on the TIMSS Video Study tape that is included in the TIMSS Achieving Excellence Toolkit. These six lessons, two each from German, Japanese, and American eighth grade classes, come with a comprehensive moderator's guide (see #13 on page 125) and serve as powerful catalysts for discussion at department and faculty meetings. It is hard to view these tapes without being struck by the differences in approach found on the tapes. Additional videotapes that model standards-based instruction at the elementary, middle, and high school levels are readily available from the Annenburg Mathematics Video Library.* Once teachers see the value of using videotapes and once they are comfortable sharing their successes and failures, actual videotapes of classroom instruction from one's own school are often the most powerful way to engage teachers and others in discussion about what is being done, what isn't being done, and what could be done to improve instruction. Regardless of how intrusive this strategy can be, we must recognize that while curriculum and assessment can be written down and shared, instruction can only be observed as it is occurring or captured for later viewing on tape.

Assessment Shifts

Finally, the glue that holds the entire system of curriculum and instruction together is the content and format of the assessment used to evaluate whether or not things are working and how well they are working. If curriculum and instruction are to change in ways that have been described here, then assessment must change as well. When the emphasis of the mathematics curriculum moves toward concepts and problem solving, a parallel move must occur in the assessments used to measure student achievement. Similarly, when the emphasis of mathematics instruction shifts toward connections and communication, in addition to correct answers, a parallel shift must occur in the assessments that teachers and school use. That is why NCTM has advocated a shift in the vision of evaluation toward a system based on evidence from multiple sources and away from relying on evidence from a single test as well as a shift toward relying on the professional judgments of teachers and away from using only externally derived evidence.

In such a coherent system in which curriculum, instruction, and assessment are closely aligned with one another one finds:

- good instruction that naturally incorporates assessment of understanding and good assessment that naturally provides opportunity to further instruct;
- ongoing informal assessment of student understanding through observations, interviews, and questioning; and

---

*More information on the Annenburg Mathematics Library is available at www.learner.org/collections/mathsci/teachers.

Traditional (easy):   Find the perimeter of this figure:

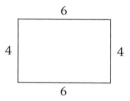

Traditional (harder):   Find the perimeter of this figure:

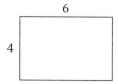

Alternative: You have 20 cm of ribbon. Use your ruler to design and draw a rectangular card that uses all the ribbon as a border. Then identify the length of each side of the card and the perimeter of your card.

Figure 3-8 Assessing an understanding of perimeter

- a system of formal assessment—quizzes, tests, extended tasks, projects, and portfolios—that closely reflects both what has been taught and how it has been taught.

Once again, to clarify expectations and to effectively advocate for change, principals and other school leaders are urged to use practical examples in the forms of exemplary assessments and student work to communicate the essence of these changes. Figure 3-8 shows two distinctly different ways of assessing students' understanding of perimeter. One asks for merely an answer and tells us little about understanding. The other looks for a solution and seeks to determine the depth of students' understanding *in addition to* an answer.

When students correctly answer the traditional questions, one is left wondering what they really understand. Do they merely know that perimeter means "add up all the numbers around" or do they have an understanding that the perimeter of a figure is the distance around the outside of the figure? And even worse, when students incorrectly answer the traditional questions, do they truly have a misunderstanding of perimeter, or have they made a minor computation error, or have they merely confused the words *area* and *perimeter*? None of these questions need to be asked when examining student work on the alternative task. Notice too that the alternative task links the concept of perimeter to the idea of border and only assesses an understanding of the vocabulary ("then find the perimeter of your card") *after* the basic conceptual understanding is established. In addition, note that the alternative task calls on students to perform (design and draw) as well as to use tools (ruler) and materials (string or ribbon), thereby giving more students access to the task and a better opportunity to demonstrate what they know and can do.

These issues of assessing the depth of understanding and ensuring an alignment between how mathematics is taught and how it is assessed is evident in Figure 3-9 in which a traditional exercise-like problem with one correct answer is compared to an alternative performance task with multiple solutions and numerous opportunities to assess real understanding of the concept of percentage in a realistic context. Notice that the ability to

---

Traditional: What is the cost of a $50 sweater that is on sale at 25% off?

Alternative: At a department store sale, you are buying a $50 sweater that you selected from a table that says "25% OFF." You also have a coupon for an additional 10% off on any purchase.

Sunday, December 23   10–5

Take an additional

10% OFF EVERYTHING

in the store*

*For example:

Regular price:	$60.00
Less the original 25% discount:	$45.00
Less an additional 10% discount:	$39.00

The cashier takes 25% off the original price and then takes an additional 10% off. She asks you for $33.75. Write what you would explain to the cashier to justify why this price is not as good as the bargain in the coupon.

Figure 3-9 Assessing an understanding of percentage

correctly complete the traditional task does *not* imply the ability to correctly solve the performance task. However, students who correctly solve the performance task must demonstrate the skill required for the traditional task, and then must demonstrate so much more.

The "What's on the Test" Strategy

One approach that teachers and administrators can use to examine current assessment practices is to gather recently administered mathematics tests that teachers have given to their students. This is an effective and straightforward approach for examining how close or how far the assessment tools being used are from the goals being professed. Because what we actually put on our tests and expect students to do best communicates what we deem to be important, a collection of tests gives unequaled insight into what is indeed valued in practice. So consider organizing faculty, grade-level, or department meetings around discussion of what appears on the mathematics tests given during, for example, the past two months. Questions one can ask about these tests include:

- What is the balance between short-answer questions and constructed-response questions in which students must show their work and explain their reasoning?

- What aspects of the curriculum must have been memorized in order for students to do well on these tests?

- What, if any, are the contexts used to engage students' interest in these tests?

- What can be inferred about the methods of instruction that preceded the test?

Two Forms of Coherence

Finally, when advocating for these changes in curriculum, instruction, and assessment, it is imperative that principals and other school leaders are aware of the systemic coherence that emerges from the two distinct sets of assumptions we are dealing with. So in the tried and true "if-then" logic of the mathematician, let me summarize the implications that arise from a traditional view and from a more reformist view.

If one believes that

- mathematical skills are the primary component of a mathematics program;

- mathematical competence is not expected of all students; and

- mathematics is an appropriate social and economic sorter of humanity;

Then it follows that

- a rigid system of tracking would be instituted;
- students would be denied access to more advanced levels of study;
- one would value teaching that took the form of telling and showing;
- applications would only be used after skills had been developed;
- technology would be approached with great caution; and
- multiple-choice tests and a focus on the right answer would predominate classroom expectations.

If, however, one believes that

- mathematics is appropriate and necessary for all students;
- problem solving and applications are the primary goals of the mathematics program; and
- mathematics is a social and economic empowerer;

Then, very differently, we would expect that

- there would be less sorting and tracking of students;
- all students would be expected to study algebra, geometry, and elements of calculus;
- more group work during class would be evident as students collaborate;
- teachers would rely less on lectures;
- one would see less emphasis on skills and more reliance on technology;
- students would regularly be confronted with the question "Why?" and challenged to suggest alternative approaches and different solutions; and
- performance tasks, scored holistically, would take the place of short-answer, percentage-correct tests.

How do these different forms of coherence play out in real classrooms? Figure 3-10 clarifies the extraordinary differences between the traditional, show-tell-practice approach to teaching mathematics and the engage-discover-connect-apply approach. It is difficult to understand how any caring parent or citizen would opt for the limited success that the traditional approach has achieved over the excitement and understanding forged by the alternative approach. Ask yourself whether you really believe that subjecting twenty-first-century students to the regurgitation of

The Traditional Approach

The teacher informs students that today's lesson will focus on finding the volume of right circular cylinders. The teacher directs students to open their books to the appropriate page and then draws on the board: (1) a picture of a right circular cylinder very similar to one pictured in the book, and (2) the formula $V = \pi r^2 h$. The teacher then places numbers on the diagram (usually without units) for the radius and height and proceeds to calculate the volume by plugging in the values for r and h into the formula. After the volume has been calculated and students have been given the chance to ask questions, the teacher assigns two practice problems that are essentially the same as the one done on the board. The students work individually, in preparation for their homework assignment that includes five more similar problems and two applications. In such a manner, a large proportion of mathematics is "taught," regurgitated back on a quiz, and quickly forgotten.

An Alternative Approach

The teacher begins class by holding up an empty soda can and asks students to work in pairs and find five mathematically appropriate ways of answering the question: About how big is this can?

After a few minutes, the teacher asks for, and records on the board, the various answers that students propose. (For example, about 5 inches high, about 10 centimeters across or in diameter, about 9 inches around, about 25 cubic inches, about 300 milliliters, etc.) The teacher then asks each proposer to use a ruler and try to convince the class—using the actual can—that their estimate is reasonable.

The teacher leads the discussion toward the fact that it is often important to know (or be able to figure out) the "volume" of a container—that is, the amount of space inside the container. Often this can be connected to previous work on volume and the fact that volume has already been seen as the "area of the base times the height." This discussion and the previous student contributions should help the class to deduce the formula for calculating the exact volume of the soda can, which in turn can be validated by the 355-milliliter capacity noted on the can.

To practice and reinforce these new understandings, students, working in pairs, are asked to calculate the volume of selected, found, or distributed cylinders (for example, a pencil, a CD, other cans, barrels, etc.) and report their findings to the class. Homework is then drawn from the *Guiness Book of World Records* from which students calculate the volume of such records as the world's largest cookie, the world record for pancake consumption, or the world's largest noodle, and then connect that volume with a familiar object to provide some sense of the magnitude of the record.

Figure 3-10 A comparison of the traditional and alternative approaches

procedures to arrive at correct answers could possibly prepare them for the world we currently inhabit, let alone the one that is emerging. Then, ask yourself whether the search for solutions and focus on explanations that characterize the alternative approach could possibly do harm.

It is important to recognize that the magnitude of the reform being advocated entails significant adjustment of the entire system. Fine-tuning only one or two aspects of the system tends to create incompatibilities that short-circuit the program and leave teachers and students frustrated. More on this subject of the components of a coherent program is presented in Chapter 7.

In summary, if we continue to do what we have always done, it shouldn't be surprising that we'll continue to get what we've always gotten. However, if what we've always gotten is no longer good enough, then the same logic that mathematicians are often so proud to rely on suggests fairly strongly that we've got to change what we've always done. At its core, this means a set of curriculum, instructional, and assessment shifts that give us a real shot at getting a lot more and lot better than we've always gotten. Anything less shortchanges students, undermines fairness, and jeopardizes our future.

4 Building Sensible, Sense-Making Mathematics: What to Encourage and Implement

One way to characterize the end result of the shifts described in Chapter 3 is as *sensible, sense-making mathematics*. Sensible mathematics is mathematics that is reasonable and rational in a technologically driven world. Understanding and knowing when and why to use the operation of division is sensible mathematics. However, being able to perform long division with two- and three-digit decimal divisors is no longer sensible mathematics. Sense-making mathematics is the mathematics of rules, procedures, techniques, and concepts that make sense to students; that is, mathematics that "feels right" and "fits together" because students have been given multiple and diverse opportunities to develop understanding. Merely showing students the rules for calculating the three cases of percentage (what is x% of y, x is what percentage of y, and x% of what is y) is not sense-making mathematics.

The Characteristics of Sensible, Sense-Making Mathematics

I believe that there are eight critical characteristics of sensible, sense-making mathematics:

Access: Sensible, sense-making mathematics is taught in an environment that gives students access to mathematics and invites them to learn.

Learning: Sensible, sense-making mathematics is taught in ways that use alternative approaches and multiple representations to develop understanding among students with diverse learning styles.

Skills: Sensible, sense-making mathematics acknowledges that there is a rational set of skills that all students need to master, but that many of the skills once considered essential are today obsolete and must be purged from the curriculum.

Tasks: Sensible, sense-making mathematics makes extensive use of high-quality instructional and assessment tasks to introduce, develop, reinforce, connect, and assess understanding of key mathematical concepts.

Language: Sensible, sense-making mathematics relies on language—both oral and written—to support the development of mathematical understanding in language-rich classrooms.

Integration: Sensible, sense-making mathematics is taught in ways that consistently connect the mathematics being learned to other mathematical ideas as well as to other disciplines.

Coherence: Sensible, sense-making mathematics is taught within coherent programs in which curriculum, instruction, professional development, community expectations, and assessment are aligned and mutually supportive.

Thinking: Sensible, sense-making mathematics is part of a thinking curriculum, as opposed to a parroting curriculum, in which "Why?" and "How do you know?" are pervasive questions in all teacher-student and student-student interchanges.

This chapter describes what each of these characteristics looks like in practice so that principals and other school leaders can encourage people to think about and implement each of these aspects of a high-quality mathematics program.

Access

I often visualize the ideal mathematics curriculum as an incredibly delicious smorgasbord laid out on a beautifully decorated table. However, it doesn't take many conversations about mathematics to quickly learn that, for many, this same smorgasbord is a noxious, rotting, unappealing array of horribly distasteful stuff. The perceived unpleasantness of the mathematics table begins to emerge as early as second grade for many students. That is when the "one-right-regrouping-approach" to get the "one-right-answer" to subtraction with regrouping worksheets brings sense-making mathematics to a screeching halt.

Instead of contributing to this aversion, curriculum and instruction must invite students at all levels to the wonderful world of mathematics by providing intellectual, emotional, and social access to the mathematics. Four tried-and-true approaches to providing access—in a sense luring students to the table of mathematics—are

- putting the mathematics into relevant and interesting **contexts;**
- encouraging the use of **technology** to remove the tedium from certain traditional aspects of mathematics;

- allowing students to **collaborate** as they explore mathematics; and
- making full use of **materials** whenever hands-on experiences can concretize mathematics.

Figures 4-1, 4-2, and 4-3 show elementary, middle, and high school tasks, respectively, that employ everyday contexts, expect that students will be using calculators, and are well suited for cooperative learning settings. In addition to the rich and important mathematics embedded in each of these tasks, each has the potential to effectively invite students into the world of mathematics and by its very nature forestalls the common "When are we ever going to need this?" question. It is critical that all who question the need for or value of a significantly reformed mathematics program consider the qualitative differences between a mathematics of practicing multiplication and division and the mathematics that arises when ordering sufficient food for a picnic; or between a page of decontextualized measurement problems and the series of questions that arise from the world record for pancake consumption; or between the rules for using logarithms

---

Traditional: Solve the following problems:

1. What is the cost of 5 cans of beans if each can costs $0.79?
2. What is the cost of 16 boxes of cereal if each box costs $2.69?
3. How much change will Sally get if she pays for 8 pounds of chicken that costs $1.89 per pound with a $20 bill?
4. How many boxes of rice, each costing $1.59, can Ron purchase if he has one $10 bill?

Alternative: Your class does some research and finds out that

- hot dogs come in packages of 8 hot dogs for $2.50;
- hot dog rolls come in packages of 6 for $0.90 and 12 for $1.50;
- hamburgers come in packages of 8 patties for $4.00; and
- hamburger buns come in packages of 8 for $1.00 and 12 for $1.65.

You expect that 24 students and 6 adults will come to the picnic you are planning. You also expect that most—but not all—students will have a hot dog and most of the adults will have a hamburger. Decide how many packages of each you should buy, find the cost of the food, explain why you made your decisions, and show how you arrived at the cost.

Figure 4-1 Traditional and alternative elementary school mathematics problems

Traditional: Solve the following problems:

1. If a man runs 5 miles per hour, how many feet per second does he run?
2. Find the product: $2\frac{3}{4} \times 5 =$
3. Find the volume of a right circular cylinder with a height of 15 inches and a diameter of 4 inches.

Alternative: The World Record for Pancake Consumption!!!

According to the *Guinness Book of World Records*, Peter Dowdeswell of London, England, holds the world record for pancake consumption!

1. What additional information would you like to know? (how many? how big? how long did it take?)

The record is 62 pancakes, each 6 inches in diameter and 3/8-inch thick with butter and syrup consumed in 6 minutes 58.5 seconds!

2. Show with your hands how high a stack that would be.
3. Exactly how high a stack would that be? (Why would the actual height of the stack probably be less?)
4. About how fast are the pancakes consumed? (pancakes per minute? pancakes per second?)
5. What is the volume of the pancakes consumed? (Is this more or less than a cubic foot?)
6. If the average human stomach is only about 125 cubic inches, how did Peter Dowdeswell set the record?
7. What would the radius of a single 3/8-inch thick pancake have to be to contain the same volume as the stack that Dowdeswell consumed?
8. Draw a graph that shows Dowdeswell's progress as he set the record.

Figure 4-2 Traditional and alternative middle school mathematics problems

to solve an exponential equation and the insights garnered from an investigation of the increase in first-class postage rates. One approach leaves far too many choking on bones and enduring a bitter aftertaste for years, the other serves as an enticing appetizer that encourages students to begin struggling with mathematical ideas. It's a no-brainer which approach entrenches the status quo and which approach recognizes that the Nintendo generation needs to be treated differently.

Traditional:

Solve for x: $3(1 + x)^{68} = 33$

Alternative:

- In 1931 first-class postage was 3¢ for the first ounce.
- In 1999 first-class postage was 33¢ for the first ounce.

1. Describe the magnitude of the increase in the cost of first-class postage between 1931 and 1999 in four different ways. Be sure that at least one of the ways includes a percentage and another includes an annual compounded growth rate.
2. Explain or show how you arrived at each way of describing the increase.

Figure 4-3 Traditional and alternative high school mathematics problems

Learning

One of the scariest realities all teachers face is the fact that at any given moment, in any given class, it's very likely that more than half of our students are neither understanding nor processing the mathematics being taught in the same way their teachers are processing it. Call it learning styles or alternative modes of learning, it comes down to different brains working in different ways. When students are asked to visualize "one quarter," one sees one-fourth of a pizza pie shaded, and another sees only the numbers one over four. Another student sees a quarter with George Washington on one side and an eagle on the other. Still another is far more comfortable with the small mark on his or her ruler between zero and one, but closer to zero, and yet another sees the mark on a measuring cup between zero and one-half.

Similarly, although we may be perfectly comfortable with the symbolic abstraction of a linear function, some of our students need the spreadsheet or tabular representation of the same equation, and still others see the line that represents the function on the coordinate plane.

Just think how often teachers think or hear: "They just don't get it!" That's why effective teachers never rely on the *one* right way to do a problem. And that's why effective teachers encourage alternative approaches and employ multiple representations of key concepts to broaden the likelihood of understanding—even approaches and representations with which they themselves are not comfortable. Figure 4-4 conveys the richness of learning when teachers encourage students to come up with alternative approaches and then use the various approaches to help develop a stronger understanding of the connections among diverse mathematical

Party Favors

Sandra is interested in buying party favors for the friends she is inviting to her birthday party. The price of the fancy straws she wants is 12 cents for 20 straws. The storekeeper is willing to split a bundle of straws for her. She wants 35 straws. How much will they cost?

Solution 1:

xxxxx xxxxx — 6¢   I drew a picture and
xxxxx xxxxx — 6¢   found that the straws
xxxxx xxxxx — 6¢   will cost 21 cents.
xxxxx   — 3¢

Solution 2:

Money	Straws
3¢	5
6¢	10
9¢	15
12¢	20
15¢	25
18¢	30
21¢	35

I solved it by making a table.

Solution 3: I thought 20 ÷ 4 = 5 and 12 ÷ 4 = 3 so 5 straws for 3¢. 7 groups of 5 will cost 21¢.

Solution 4: Since 20 straws cost 12¢, you can get 10 straws for 6¢ and 5 for 3¢.
So since 20 + 10 + 5 is 35, it will cost 12 + 6 + 3 or 21¢.

Solution 5: One bundle has 20 straws. You want 35, or 15 more straws.
15 straws is ¾ of a bundle, so they will cost ¾ of 12 or 9¢.
All 35 will then cost 12 + 9 or 21¢.

Solution 6: 12 is to 20 as *x* is to 35. Cross multiply (12 × 35) and divide by 20.
So 420 ÷ 20 = 21 and the straws will cost 21¢.

Solution 7: If 20 straws cost 12¢, each straw will cost 12 ÷ 20 or .6¢ per straw.
35 straws × .6¢ per straw = 21¢.

Figure 4-4 Seven alternative solutions to the same problem

representations. The problem in Figure 4-4 also demonstrates that, even when students are given a rather insipid and thoroughly unreasonable problem, there is still ample opportunity for great instruction if discussion moves beyond the correct answer and toward alternative approaches.

Consider how easy it is to strengthen instruction by engaging students, as well as colleagues, in discussions that employ alternative approaches and multiple representations (e.g., a table, a proportion, or a picture) to foster better understanding and help broaden teachers' repertoire of strategies.

Another aspect of learning that we all recognize, but seldom talk about, is how rare it is to teach a perfect class and how common it is to make mistakes. In fact, we know that it is almost impossible to teach a 45-minute class without making at least two mistakes. Usually, one mistake is mathematical and careless because we're thinking two steps ahead. Sometimes our students catch our mistakes and sometimes the errors sit on the board unnoticed until no one agrees with the final answer. The second mistake is usually pedagogical and results from calling on the wrong student at the wrong time or assigning the wrong problem at the wrong time—engendering far more confusion than we'd prefer.

To make this worse, we've learned that when a principal or supervisor is in the room, we significantly increase the likelihood of an additional mistake. And if we're using technology, it's essentially impossible to avoid hitting the wrong key at least once! Yet mistakes are often how we all learn best. They prepare us for a world that regularly expects people to "debug" situations, and they force us to reanalyze our thinking. If understanding is the goal of all learning, then focusing on alternative approaches, multiple representations, and debugging mistakes and errors are three powerful instructional tools for strengthening understanding of mathematics.

Skills

A large proportion of the controversy surrounding the reform and improvement of mathematics programs centers on skills. Many of the debates regarding what is still "baby" and what is increasingly "bath water" focus on skills. Yet what is clear is that some skills are as important, if not more important, than ever. Other skills remain in the curriculum only because of tradition.

A brief list of essential mathematical skills is not difficult to generate. For example, there is little disagreement that all students must have a command of one-digit number facts. Students need to be able to estimate sums, differences, products, and quotients. There is widespread agreement that using various tools to measure and being able to create graphs from data presented in tables and charts are important skills, and the list grows on.

However, an amazing amount of time and energy is still expended—by teachers and their students—on increasingly obsolete skills, that is, skills no longer valued by society. Policy makers, parents, and test developers need to give educators permission to skip textbook pages that no longer serve a useful purpose. Among those skills that should be relegated to the "bath water" are

- paper-and-pencil multiplication problems with two-digit or larger factors (three digits by one digit should be enough);
- paper-and-pencil division problems with two-digit or larger divisors (four digits by one digit should be enough); and
- computation with fractions with unreasonable denominators like sevenths or ninths (halves, fourths, eighths; thirds and sixths; fifths and tenths should be enough).

The importance of retaining appropriate skills in the curriculum should now be clear. It is equally important to provide ongoing practice of these important skills. Almost no one masters something new after one or two lessons and one or two homework assignments. That's why one of the most effective strategies for fostering retention and mastery is *daily, cumulative review* at the beginning of every class. Some teachers call it warmups, others call it daily mini-math. Some days it's delivered orally, other days it's written on the broad or shown on the overhead. But everyday it's a few quick problems to keep skills sharp. And everyday teachers present something similar to

- a **fact** of the day (e.g., 7×6);
- an **estimate** of the day (e.g., If one item costs 32¢ and another costs 29¢, about how much will it cost to buy both items?);
- a **measurement** of the day (e.g., About how many meters wide is our classroom?);
- a **place value** problem of the day (e.g., What number is 100 more than 1,584?);
- a **word problem** of the day; and
- any other exercises or problems that reinforce weaker, newer, or needed skills and concepts.

Tasks

As mathematics instruction shifts from skills to concepts and from exercises to problems, tasks have begun to replace examples as the building block of good instruction. Tasks—often referred to as performance activities—are used to engage students in thinking about and learning mathematical ideas. The tasks with which students are engaged provide rich opportunities for students to be active and to perform—as they struggle to grasp important mathematical ideas. As described in NCTM's *Professional Standards for Teaching Mathematics*, good tasks provide students with opportunities "to reason about mathematical ideas, to make connections, and to formulate, grapple with and solve problems. Good tasks test skill development in the context of problem solving, are accessible to students, and promote communication about mathematics" (pp. 24–25).

I have found it useful to conceptualize powerful tasks as *performance activities* that constitute opportunities to be *doing mathematics* (solving problems) in *situations* (a context, specific givens, and goals) for a *purpose* (human goals and a definable audience).

Additionally, I believe that three overarching premises help us create and adapt high-quality mathematics performance tasks:

1. Mathematics is everywhere.

2. Good mathematics arises naturally from everyday situations and data.

3. Good mathematical tasks arise in turn from the human questions that are generated by these situations and data.

The following are among the human questions that often open the floodgates to good mathematical experiences:

- Could that be?

- Is that reasonable?

- Is that fair?

- Really?

In addition to stealing good tasks from textbooks and supplemental materials, good instructional and assessment tasks tend to emerge in two ways. One approach begins with data of some sort that originate in newspapers, magazines, menus, price lists, catalogs, sports, almanacs, world records, etc. Teachers and other task developers train themselves to ask where is the important mathematics in these data and what are the questions that elicit this mathematics. A second approach begins with a chunk of mathematics that is to be taught. In this case, teachers and other task developers train themselves to ask when and where do normal human beings use such mathematics and how can these uses be translated into engaging tasks.

For example, Figure 4-5 begins with a commonly found price list for different sizes of ladders. The questions posed reveal how the data can be "mined" for tasks that deal with such mathematical ideas as unit costs, the

---

Ladder Pricing

The Sunday newspaper circulars include the following chart in an advertisement for ladders:

Size	Cost
16′	$36
20′	$58
24′	$75
28′	$99
32′	$130

1. Calculate the unit price for each ladder and explain why you think the unit price changes as it does.
2. Suppose that there were a demand for a 22-foot ladder. Propose an appropriate cost for such a ladder and explain how you arrived at your proposal.
3. Suppose that the top of the highest window on a house is 18 feet above ground level and that for safety reasons all ladders should be placed at an angle of 75° to the ground. Which of the five ladders would be most appropriate for you to purchase? Explain how you arrived at your decision.
4. It is obvious from the chart that the longer the ladder, the mort costly it is. Find a relationship between, or a formula that links, the length of the ladder in feet and the cost of the ladder in dollars that could be used to arrive at a price for all lengths of ladders. Build a convincing argument for your relationship or formula.

Figure 4-5 How to "mine" tasks from everyday data

trigonometry of ladder angles, and the algebraic modeling of determining the cost C for each ladder as a function of length L.

Alternatively, Figure 4-6 is an example of creating a situation to help develop skill, in this case, an understanding of surface area. Asking under what circumstances a person might have a need to understand surface area results in the creation of this hospital setting that requires estimating how much skin or surface an average human has.

Regardless of the method used to develop tasks, Figure 4-7 suggests a set of characteristics for all performance tasks that emerged from Connecticut's Common Core of Learning Mathematics Assessment Project.

A Lot of Skin in the Game

Overheard in the E.R.:

"Oh my god, he's completely burned from head to toe!"

"Not a problem. Just order up 1,000 square inches of skin from the graft bank."

You could respond:

A. "Oh, good, that'll be enough to cover it." or B. "Oh, oh, the patient's in a lot of trouble here."

1. Which response (A or B) is more appropriate?
2. Explain how you decided.
3. About how much skin would *you* order to be sure you have enough?
4. Explain how you arrived at your estimate.

Figure 4-6 Creating a situation to develop understanding of a concept

---

Essential (not tangential): a focus on "big ideas"

Authentic (not contrived): directly involves meaningful uses of mathematics, not artificially constrained

Equitable (not biased): gives diverse students access; mathematics not hidden behind culturally exclusive information

Rich (not simplistic): numerous possibilities and solution paths lead naturally to other questions and problems

Engaging (not uninteresting): thought provoking; fosters persistence

Active (not passive): student is worker and decision maker; student interacts with other students

Accessible (not inaccessible): a context that is inviting; students with diverse ability can work actively and productively

---

Figure 4-7 Characteristics of high-quality performance tasks

Language

We often talk about mathematics as a language. Certainly, it is a language, complete with elements, notation, and syntax. A little less literally, mathematics is the language of patterns and the language of change. A little more poetically, in words attributed to Galileo, "mathematics is the pen God used to write the universe." But more practically, language is a powerful tool for developing mathematical understanding. When students articulate their answers or explain their reasoning orally, or when they show their work and "write up" their conclusions, they are using language to develop and demonstrate understanding. In fact, it is nearly impossible to teach mathematics to students who cannot read, and it is extremely difficult to assess the mathematical understanding of students who cannot speak or write. This is why the notions of communication (oral and written) and discourse (between student and teacher, and among students) have become such important components of improving mathematics programs. And this is why the notion of interactive, language-rich classrooms is so compelling.

Several pieces of student work that capture these ideas are presented in Chapter 5. For now however, Figures 4-8 and 4-9 model the use of oral and written language, respectively, and demonstrate again the difference between a language-poor, correct-answer approach and a language-rich, thinking, and probing approach.

Integration

When a program is integrated, the material being taught is connected to material previously taught and to material that will be taught in the future. In addition, and very importantly, these connections are made both within and across disciplines. Integrating mathematics, both within mathematics and with other subject areas, is one of the most difficult aspects of reform. However, a mathematics that ignores these connections isolates mathematics in ways never found outside of school.

Two strategies for increasing the links within mathematics and between subject areas are focusing on alternative approaches and relying on interesting contexts—both of which were discussed earlier in this chapter. Figures 4-10, 4-11, and 4-12 provide three relatively straightforward situations that naturally open the door to connections with other areas of study while still providing rich opportunities to do mathematics.

Coherence

Nothing is more demoralizing than to confront high-stakes tests that do not match the instructional materials that are available and in use. Little is more unprofessional than forcing teachers to participate in professional development on topics and with tools that are not yet available when

---

Traditional approach: Find the difference: 82 – 48

Alternative approach: For the number sentence: 82 – 48 = ❐

1. Make up a problem using realistic data and a common situation that would require someone to find this difference.

2. What is a reasonable estimate for a solution to your problem?

3. Explain how you arrived at your estimate.

4. What is the exact answer to your problem?

5. Explain how you arrived at this answer.

6. Did anyone use a different approach to solve this problem? What did you do?

Figure 4-8 Language-poor and language-rich: An oral approach

teachers return to their classrooms. And little is more confusing to students than having to cope with disconnections between *what* they are expected to learn, *how* they are expected to learn it, and *how* this material is assessed. Yet these types of misalignment regularly infiltrate mathematics programs and undermine both teaching and learning.

Traditional:

If the average 18-year-old is reported to have witnessed 40,000 made-for-TV murders, how many murders does the average American child witness each day?

Alternative:

Following the spate of violent acts in schools, the president announced that "the typical American child has witnessed 40,000 murders on TV by the time he or she is 18."

Survey your classmates and gather whatever data you believe is necessary to assess the reasonableness of the president's claim. Then write a letter to the president explaining how your investigation affirms or rebuts his claim.

Figure 4-9 Language-poor and language-rich: A written approach

Stimulus:

1994 Population by Continent

North America	289,000,000
South America	474,000,000
Europe	509,000,000
Asia	3, 344,000,000
Africa	701,000,000
Former USSR	296,000,000
Oceania	28,000,000

Nonmathematical connections:

1. Where are these continents located on the globe?
2. Are there any continents missing from this list? Why?
3. What do the most populous continents have in common?

Mathematical possibilities:

1. Order the continents by population.
2. What fractional part of the world's total population reside in each continent?

Figure 4-10 Population problem integrating geography and mathematics

Two forms of coherence were proposed in Chapter 3, one capturing the coherence of the traditional approach and the other capturing an alternative, more appropriate approach. It bears repeating that *if* one believes that mathematics is appropriate and necessary for all students, that problem solving and applications are the primary goals of the mathematics program, and that mathematics must be a social and economic empower, *then* it would follow, in a coherent program, that:

- there would be less sorting and tracking of students;
- all students would be expected to study algebra, geometry, and elements of calculus;
- more group work would be found during class as students collaborate more;
- teachers would rely less on lecture;
- one would see less emphasis on skills and more reliance on technology;
- students would regularly be confronted with the question "Why?" and challenged to suggest alternative approaches and different solutions; and

---

Stimulus: A *USA Today* snippet announcing that a new $100 bill with a bigger, offset picture of Benjamin Franklin and several innovations to thwart counterfeiting goes into circulation today. So far $80 billion worth has been printed, equal to about ⅔ of all old $100 bills in use.

Nonmathematical connections:

1. Vocabulary—offset, innovation, thwart, counterfeiting
2. Who is Benjamin Franklin? Why is he pictured on the $100 bill?
3. What other bill has the picture of someone who never served as president?
4. Why do you think the government is changing the design of our currency?
5. What other contexts are there for "circulation"? What does it mean for money to circulate?

Mathematical possibilities:

1. How many bills are represented by the $80 billion?
2. How many $100 bills are in circulation all together?
3. How large a container would be needed to store all $80 billion worth of new bills?

Figure 4-11 Monetary problem integrating vocabulary, history, current events, and mathematics

- performance tasks scored holistically would take the place of short-answer, percentage-correct tests.

Thinking

Probably the best way to implement a thinking curriculum, to help focus on alternative approaches, and to create a language-rich classroom, is by regularly asking *"Why?" "How do you know?"* or *"Can you explain what you did and why you did it?"* A student who can explain his or her answer usually has a stronger understanding of mathematics. Classrooms where students are regularly explaining how and why—in groups and in whole-class discussions—help other students learn mathematics. That's why nearly every exhibit and example in this book asks for more than a numerical answer. That's why multiple-choice testing must give way to more open-ended, constructed response assessment. And that is why one of the most beneficial practices in any classroom is monitoring how often

---

Stimulus:
Heard on NPR's *All Things Considered*: Every cigarette you smoke reduces your life by 7 minutes!

Nonmathematical connections:
Why is cigarette smoking harmful?

Mathematical possibilities:
Is this claim reasonable? Convince yourself that it is.

Interdisciplinary task:
Use the data given by NPR about reduction in life expectancy and write what you believe would be a compelling advertisement that might convince teenagers not to smoke.

Figure 4-12 Cigarette smoking problem integrating science, expository writing, and mathematics

the word *why* is uttered—not just when incorrect answers are given, but when any answer is proposed.

A Strategy for Elevating These Components

A department, school, or community seeking to implement sensible, sense-making mathematics programs like those described in this chapter can elevate the presence of each of these components by incorporating attention to each of them in all discussions pertaining to the mathematics program. Whether in discussions about the curriculum, instruction, or assessment; whether as part of discussions about videotapes or student work; or whether as part of teacher evaluation or the selection of new materials; principals and other school leaders should channel people's thinking to these issues of access, learning, skills, tasks, language, integration, coherence, and thinking.

5 *Pulling It All Together: Glimpses of What We Should See*

It's one thing to talk about transforming curriculum and instruction and about sensible, sense-making mathematics, it's quite another to put it in place and recognize when it's taking place. So let's turn to what reform looks like and feels like in the classroom. Here is what any observer of mathematics instruction should expect to see:

Classrooms are active environments—often noisy, but clearly productive and purposeful—as students converse mathematically and wrestle with ideas in the course of solving interesting problems. It is unlikely that desks are in rows or that the teacher spends a significant proportion of class time at the chalkboard. Instead, desks are likely to be clustered in groups of three, four, or five, and calculators and other appropriate materials are readily available and being used.

Teachers are likely to be found conferring with a group of students, asking probing questions, launching an activity, drawing out conjectures, stimulating discussion of findings, or summarizing the big ideas and conclusions reached by different groups. There may be traditional lecture at times as teachers clarify ideas and concepts, but more often, the teacher is coaching, selecting, and orchestrating tasks, setting high expectations, and encouraging high levels of thinking and reasoning.

Similarly, no longer just passive absorbers of lecture and regurgitaters of procedures, **students** clearly assume greater responsibility for their own learning. One can see students actively engaged in doing and learning mathematics—measuring, counting, graphing, modeling, generalizing, and solving. They expect to struggle at times and bask in a sense of accomplishment at others, as they gradually come to see mathematics as a living discipline and a powerful set of tools and ideas, rather than merely a collection of rules that get memorized for a test and just as quickly are forgotten.

Homework assignments are rarely pages of mindless exercises; instead, they are opportunities to engage students in problems that build on work done in class, that relate to students' own lives and interests, or that involve collecting data and other information that will be used in class. Similarly, **tests and quizzes** are no longer given only at the end of a unit of instruction, but are embedded parts of instruction and are often replaced with projects, classwork, and homework. All this results in **grades** that are based on a multiple sources of information and that reflect a more complete view of students' understanding of mathematics.

From Tasks to Student Work: Artifacts of Mathematics That Are Working

Once again, however, we have resorted to words to describe the vision of a reform-based mathematics classroom. To better crystallize this vision, teachers have increasingly used student work as artifacts of sensible, sense-making mathematics. Principals and other school leaders can easily replicate this strategy. Consider the following examples that capture engaging, concept-oriented, problem-solving approaches to mathematics. Each can be used to help illustrate the outcomes of sensible, sense-making mathematics. Each can also be used to stimulate teachers to craft instruction that generates similar examples.

Darda Cars in Annette Raphel's Class at Milton Academy in Massachusetts

When the seventh graders in Ms. Raphel's class were studying rates, similarity, and dimensional analysis, Ms. Raphel found an advertisement claiming that Darda toy cars went 520 miles per hour (scale speed)! Not surprisingly, her students found this hard to believe. Ms. Raphel saw this as a perfect opportunity to deal with issues of scale and proportionality. Figure 5-1 shows the letter the class sent to Darda, Inc. explaining their findings, and Figure 5-2 shows the equally wonderful letter the class subsequently received from Darda with more questions than answers.

TV Viewing in Ms. Cavanaugh's Class at the Gideon Welles Middle School in Connecticut

When Ms. Cavanaugh's class was studying statistics and data analysis, she gave her class the Television Viewing Habits and Their Impact task that I had designed and shared with teachers. Figure 5-3 shows the task and one piece of work completed by a student in her class.

Ice Cream Cones in Jim Cochrane's Class at Lewis Mills High School in Connecticut

Similarly, while teaching his geometry students about finding the volume of regular three-dimensional figures, Mr. Cochrane posed the following task:

MILTON ACADEMY

Darda, Inc.
USA Dock 2/1600 Union Avenue
Baltimore, MD. 21211

Dear Darda Corporation,

We are a seventh grade math class at Milton Academy and we investigated your claim that your cars go up to 520 miles per hour scaled speed. Our teacher bought two cars (item 1150) and we tested them. We had trouble in the beginning because they did not go straight, although we found long corridors to use for the testing. We had to devise tracks laid out between foam rubber and rulers.

One group found that the car went 6 feet in .9 seconds and figured out that there are 66 and 2/3 of those .9 second intervals in one minute, so therefore the car went 400 feet in one minute or 24,000 feet in one hour. We divided by 5,280 and found out that the car goes about 4.5 miles per hour. Then we measured the wheel base of our car which was 1 and 1/4 inches and measured the wheel base of a Honda Accord, which we thought was fairly standard. That was 8 feet, so we decided that it was a safe assumption that the scale of your car to a real car was 8 feet to 1 and 1/4 inches or 77 to one. We multiplied the 4.5 miles per hour by the 'scaling factor' of 77 and we concluded that the car goes a scaled speed of about 346.5 miles per hour. Looking at percent of error, we think that this is 170 miles per hour off what you had advertised (520 miles per hour), or a margin of error of about 33%!

Our other group took a number of trial runs and averaged that the car, when speeding against a bank of lockers which was 7 feet long, took about 1.05 seconds. There are 754.28 groups of 7 feet in a mile, so that means that 754.28 x 1.05 = 791.99 seconds to go one mile. That means it takes 13.19 minutes to go that one mile. 60 divided by 13.19 minutes will tell you how many miles the car can go in one hour. That group discovered that the car goes about 4.54 miles per hour. Using the same 77 to 1 ratio to account for the difference in the size of the cars, they decided that the car could travel scaled speeds of 346 miles per hour.

We were startled with how close the results were in both groups and know that although we were using good stop watches, that there were many variables which could have accounted for the discrepancy between your numbers and ours. We would like to know how you arrived at your figure. Some people hypothesized that you used a wind tunnel or just measured the speed at the first microsecond when the acceleration is at its peak. We would also like you to know how much we enjoyed using the Darda vehicles.

We are looking forward to hearing from you. Thanks for your attention.

Figure 5-1 Class letter to Darda, Inc.

You may or may not remember that the volume of a sphere is $\frac{4}{3}\pi r^3$ and the volume of a cone is $\frac{1}{3}\pi r^2 h$. Consider the Ben and Jerry's ice cream sugar cone, 8 cm in diameter and 12 cm high, capped with an 8 cm in diameter sphere of deep, luscious, decadent, rich, triple chocolate ice cream. If the ice cream melts completely, will the cone overflow or not? Explain your reasoning and show your work.

Figure 5-4 shows the work of a student in Mr. Cochrane's class and demonstrates both a depth of understanding and a strong ability to communicate mathematically, as well as a great sense of humor.

Darda Inc., U.S.A.

1600 Union Avenue. • Baltimore, Maryland 21211 • (410)-889-1023 • FAX (410)-889-0503

Dear Students:

I'm glad you enjoyed the Darda cars. A healthy scepticism of advertising claims is a good thing to have in our current culture.

Your math skills are excellent and you have clearly proven that the cars are not traveling at 520 scale miles per hour for the distance you tested them. Does this mean we are lying to you?

Did you record the maximum speed of the car or the average speed of the car? Did the conditions under which you tested your cars allow them to reach their maximum speed? What are the ideal conditions for a Darda car? (The answer is the Darda track, which should arrive at your school soon- I sent it UPS.)

Perhaps in the meantime you can consult with your science or physics teacher about your experiment and how the way you tested and measured the cars might influence the result. You might discuss:

Friction: How does it affect speed?

The difference between acceleration and speed: is the moment of maximum acceleration the same as the moment of maximum speed?

Acceleration curves- at what distance from its starting point does the Darda car reach its maximum speed?

Maximum vs. average speed.

We don't claim that no matter what you do, our cars will go 520 scale miles per hour, we claim that under their own power they can go as fast as 520 scale miles per hour.

Are we telling the truth?

Looking forward to
your reply,

Larry Grubb,
Darda R&D

Darda™

Figure 5-2 Darda, Inc.'s reply to the class letter

As a result of an instructional program in mathematics like that described in this guide, by the end of Grade 8, all students should be expected to complete work like the sample below:

TELEVISION VIEWING HABITS AND THEIR IMPACT

The following project assesses your ability to integrate and use your mathematical understandings to gather data, analyze the data and communicate your conclusions. You will have approximately two weeks to complete this project.

The following editorial appeared in your local newspaper:

TV Continues To Rot Young Minds

The evidence is clear. Study after study confirms what parents have suspected all along:

- American children watch too many hours of TV;
- American children watch too much violence on TV; and
- American children watch too many hours of cartoons.

One study suggests that, for every hour spent in school each week, the average 12 year old watches two hours of TV! Another study suggests that the typical child has seen 10,000 made-for-TV murders by age 14! And researchers have found that, by age 10, many children have already watched almost a year of cartoons!

It's time for parents to turn the TV off. It's time for children to rediscover reading and games and conversation and homework. It's time to stop the rotting of the minds of our young people.

Do you agree? Do editorials like this one make you angry? Do you believe what the studies show and the researchers mentioned in the editorial say? Well, how about doing something about it.

Your task for this project is to: **Write a detailed letter to the editor that summarizes how and why you agree or disagree with the claims made in the editorial. Your letter must be supported by data you collect from other students in your class or school. This data should then be organized into graphs or charts that should be included in your letter.**

To successfully complete this task you are expected to:

- design a survey that will allow you to test the claims made in the editorial;
- conduct the survey and gather data from at least 30 students;
- analyze the data and create some graphs or charts to display the data you have collected; and
- write a detailed letter to the editor that summarizes your findings, includes your graphs or charts, and states clearly whether or not you agree with the claims made in the editorial and why.

115

Figure 5-3 TV viewing habits task and student response

Your work will be evaluated on how well you have:

- identified the claims and gathered data to test those claims;
- organized your thoughts and used your data to argue for or against a claim or claims – that is, how good a case you make in support of or against each claim;
- used important mathematical ideas in designing your survey and analyzing your data; and
- communicated your findings effectively – both in words and graphically.

May 8, 1997

Dear Editor of the Glastonbury Citizen:

   In your recent editorial about <u>Television Viewing Habits and Their Impact: TV Continues to Rot Young Minds,</u> I totally disagree with every statistic you gave to the people of Glastonbury. But I do agree with your comments that American children watch too many hours of TV, too much violence on TV; and children watch too many hours of cartoons. In the following paragraphs I have listed statistics that are reasonable than the ones originally listed.

   In the article one study suggests that for every hour spent in school each week, the average 12-year-old watches 2 hour of TV. That says that this child witch spends about 8 hours in school is spending 16 hours watching TV when he or she gets home. I would like to know what kind of person this is! The calculator must have forgot that each child spends time studying, eating, and sleeping. I provide a graph to show the daily schedule of a 12-year-old.

Daily Schedule for a 12 year old

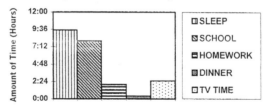

   The time in which the child could watch TV was based on the fact that he or she would get up at 7AM and get ready for school. Then they would start school at 8AM and would then be home by about 4PM.

   Once they got home, he or she could do homework, eat, or watch TV in any order for about the next 5 hrs 30 minutes until they had to go to bed at 9:30 PM. Most children go to bed about that time and don't stay up later but for the one that do I have included a couple more minutes in the graph. Maybe your stats came from aliens.

   Now, I agree with the fact that American children watch too much violence on TV. But, another study in the article suggests that the typical child has seen 10,000

Figure 5-3 (Continued)

made-for-TV murders by age 14. I disagree with this suggestion. One factor that first has to be considered is that from age 1-3 the child will not be interested in a show without songs and lots of color like a cartoon. Second, there are about 60 made-for-TV murders per month on TV. Here are the steps I followed in order to come to my conclusion.

60 TV murders (X) 12 months (X) 11 years of watching = Amount TV murders viewed

60 X 12 X 11 = 7,920 TV murders

In this area, if you were to also include all of the murder movies your number of murders could be well over 10,000 murders. But, if you don't like murder movies both the number of TV murders and movie murders would be lower. But the real violence comes from other shows like Mighty Morphing Power Rangers, or any other ninja or fighting shows. That should have been another study.

My final topic is I agree that American children watch too many hours of cartoons but disagree with the research that says that by the age of 10, children have already watched almost a year of cartoons. I say that they watch even more than that, it is about 1 year and 3 months! Here is how I came to my conclusion. I computed that at age 1, most babies aren't interested in cartoon. (I have a one-year-old brother.) But from age 2-7 one child watches about 4 hours of cartoons a day. So I then said it would take 6 days to make 24 hours of TV. Next, I divided 365 days by 6 and received 60.833. Last, I multiplied 60.833 by 24 then by 6, which stands for six years of watching cartoon.

365/6 = 60.833   60.833 x 24 = 121.666   121.666 x 6 = 8,759.9   about 8,760

Next, to figure out the amount of cartoons watched by children ages 8-10 first I divided 365 by 12 days in would take to complete 24 hrs. of TV. I figure at this age kids have more activities and are more interested in other programs. Then I multiplied that product by 24. At last, I multiplied that new product by 3 years of viewing.

365/12 = 30.416   30.416 x 24 = 729.999   729.999 x 3 = 2,189.999   about 2,190

2,190 + 8,760 = 10,950 hours of cartoons after 10 years of age
There are a only 8,760 hours in one year, so kids see a lot of bugs and daffy duck!

In conclusion, next time you print an editorial about recent statistics, please make sure they look correct so there won't be confusion and people angry with false information.

Sincerely,

Figure 5-3 (Continued)

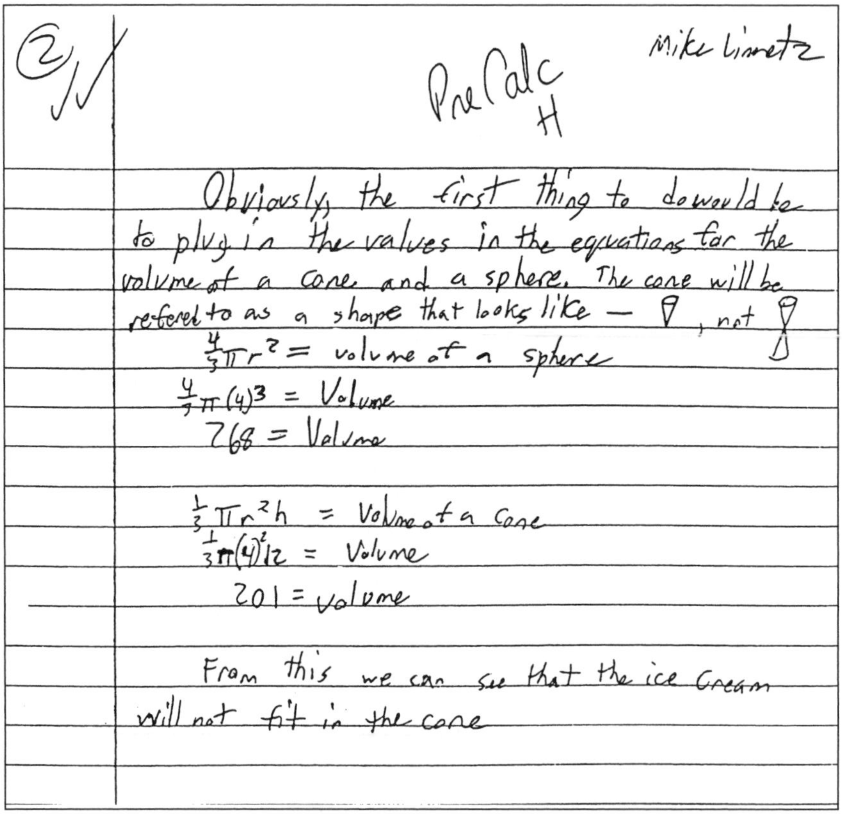

Figure 5-4 *One student's response to the ice cream cone problem*

Now I will compare the two formulas for the volume of a Cone and the volume of a sphere

sphere	Cone
$\frac{4}{3}\pi r^3$	$\frac{1}{3}\pi r^2 h$

comparison

$$\frac{4}{3}\pi r^3 \overset{?}{=} \frac{1}{3}\pi r^2 h$$

$$4\pi r^3 \overset{?}{=} \pi r^2 h$$

$$4\pi r \overset{?}{=} \pi h$$

$$4r \overset{?}{=} h$$

From this final comparison, we can see that if the height of cone is exactly 4 times the radius, then the volumes will be equal.

Now, let's try our example. The cone has a diameter of 8 and a height of 12. The sphere of Ice Cream has a diameter of 8.   Diameter 8 = radius 4

$$4(\text{radius of the sphere}) \overset{?}{=} h$$
$$4(4) \overset{?}{=} 12$$
$$16 > 12$$

Ergo, the ice cream will not fit into the cone. That concludes the mathematical reasoning section of my proof. Let us proceed to the reality section of my reasoning, shall we?

Figure 5-4 (Continued)

Many questions need to be answered as to how the ice cream will act in real life.

- Will the ice cream's volume change as it melts?
- Is it possible to compress ice cream?
- Is the ball of ice cream a perfect sphere?
- Is ice cream porous?
- Is the interior of the cone perfectly smooth?
- What kind of Ice cream is it?
    (bubble gum, chocolate chip, rocky road)
- Is there a hole at the tip of the cone?
- Why is the sky blue?

These questions and many more must be left unanswered. I do not posess the proper equipment or funds to do experiments with ice cream.
My hypothesis is that when the ice cream melts it will take up less space. I'm not sure if it will be small enough to fit inside the cone, however.

Figure 5-4 (Continued)

Burger King in Tom Kessell's Class at Antioch High School in Illinois

When the all-important percentages unit arrived in Mr. Kessell's Transition Math class, he began the unit with a "percent scavenger hunt." Each student was asked to bring "three percentages" to class—percentages found on labels, in articles, in advertisements, etc. One student arrived in class the following day with the Burger King ad that "Our Hamburgers are 75% Bigger" and the fine print that this is "by weight of uncooked hamburgers." Once again, students were startled by the apparent exaggeration in the claim. With Mr. Kessell's assistance and encouragement, the class conducted a detailed experiment and investigation into the actual differences in size between the Whopper and the Big Mac. Figures 5-5 and 5-6 contain the letter from the class to Burger King and the table of data. Figure 5-7 contains the response back from Burger King.

```
Barry J. Gibbons, CEO
Burger King
17777 Old Cutler Rd.
Miami, FL. 33157


Dear Mr. Gibbons,


                                    I am writing on behalf
of my fellow students and teacher in my Transition Math class.
In that class we have been working with percentage.
    During a discussion, your commercial, claiming that your ham
burgers have 75% more meat than those of McDonalds, came up. The
discussion turned into such a frenzy that our teacher realized
that we had an obvious interest in the subject.
    The next day we were excited to see that our teacher had
done some research. On his desk were two bags. In them were ham-
burgers, one cooked and uncooked from Burger King, and the same
from McDonalds. As we looked we were shocked. It was hard to
believe that McDonalds hamburger meat was so small compared to
yours. I was one of those doubters, so that night, I went and
did the same. What I found was no different than what we found
in class.
    The following day we did extensive testing. Weighing and
measuring the two burgers. During the testing we determined
that your burger was 80% bigger and not 75%. We were wondering
why not just say 80%?
    Our class applaudes Burger King for giving the customer
what they really want.


                        Sincere thanks,
```

Figure 5-5 Class letter to Burger King

Percents in advertising

Comparison of products

Burger King advertised that their hamburger is 75% larger than McDonald's. The advertising states that the 75% is by weight of uncooked hamburgers. The class examined one frozen and one cooked hamburger from both Burger King and McDonald's. The results are as follows:

McDonald's	Cooked		Frozen	
Diameter	3 1/8 in		3 7/8 in	
Thickness	11/32 in		1/4 in	
Volume	2.6 cu. in.		2.9 cu. in.	
Weight	27.1 grams		43.7 grams	
Burger King		% Increase		% Increase
Diameter	3 7/8 in	24%	4 5/8 in	19%
Thickness	7/16 in	27%	5/16 in	25%
Volume	5.2 cu. in.	100%	5.3 cu. in.	83%
Weight	48.8 grams	80%	79.1 grams	81%

Figure 5-6 Table comparing Burger King data and McDonald's data

American Cheese on the Pilot New York State Assessment

Finally, when building prototype tasks for a new statewide assessment, test developers in New York State opted *not* to ask students to "Express 1¾ as a decimal." Instead, students were given the following task:

> You order 1¾ pounds of American cheese. The clerk sliced the cheese, put it on the scale, and stopped when the scale read 1.34 pounds. Explain what you would say to the clerk to be sure you get the right amount of cheese.

Consider the difference between the one-right-answer question and the more open-ended task, and consider the difference in the responses each would ellict.

Here is a representative set of answers from one class:

- Turn it into a fraction.

- Wait until it says 1.75.

- 1¾ is 1.75, not 1.34 because it's 3 out of 4.

- I do not understand.

- I would say thank you, because it is the correct amount.

JAMES ADAMSON
CHIEF EXECUTIVE OFFICER

Mr. Thomas R. Kessell
Antioch Community High School
1133 Main Street
Antioch, ILL   60002-1899

Dear Mr. Russell:

I was delighted to receive your letter and read about the experiment your class conducted! To be the best hamburger restaurant in the world, we at Burger King have worked hard to ensure that we are serving our customers bigger, better hamburgers that are flame-broiled - not fried. As you and your students have seen, we are offering a far superior product to that of McDonald's.

I have enclosed Free WHOPPER® Sandwich coupons for you and your class to enjoy. Again, thank you for writing us here at Burger King.

Sincerely,

James B. Adam

James B. Adamson

BURGER KING CORPORATION • 17777 OLD CUTLER ROAD • P.O. BOX 020783 • MIAMI, FLORIDA 33102-0783
(305) 378-7770 • FAX: (305) 378-7403

Figure 5-7 Burger King's reply to class' letter

- Give me more you klutz.
- Get me someone who knows what they're doing around here.

These answers, both correct and incorrect, partial and without a clue, become a wonderful starting point for additional instruction.

The bottom line here is that our focus must be far less on what adults say and more on what students actually do. The tasks and the student work that these tasks have elicited, and that have been presented in this chapter, are the clearest indicator of whether mathematics instruction is or is not working, is or is not sensible, and is or is not resulting in student learning of important mathematical ideas. There can be little doubt that the classes in which this work was produced are representative of mathematics classes we would hope to see for all students.

6 Recognizing and Overcoming Obstacles: Insights and Practical Strategies

As I noted in the introduction, people cannot do what they cannot envision. People will not do what they don't believe is possible or can work. And people cannot do what they don't understand how to do. These three simple truisms of human nature remind us that all of the efforts to implement the changes discussed in this book must be grounded in

- creating and sharing a vision for school mathematics;

- helping people understand and envision this vision;

- showing people that reform *is* possible and *does* work; and

- broadening people's understanding so they become confident in their own ability to do things differently.

Change agents and other advocates of reform have learned that changing *behavior* requires changes in *beliefs* and in *conditions*. It also means modeling what is being advocated through demonstrations and examples. Given the magnitude of the changes we are asking teachers of mathematics to make and the obstacles these teachers face in trying to move forward, principals and other school leaders need specific strategies for providing leadership and assistance. This chapter examines some of the major obstacles to change and proposes a set of practical strategies for helping to overcome these obstacles, reduce isolation, improve conditions, inculcate a vision, change beliefs, and ultimately change behaviors.

Teachers of Mathematics Are Different

The deep, dark secret in schools is that all teachers and all schools are *not* the same. Schools *are* different and different teachers have difference strengths and different needs. In our rush to democratize our initiatives, we overlook the fact that teachers of mathematics are being asked to teach in distinctly different ways from how they themselves were taught. The magnitude of the challenge facing teachers of mathematics and, even more importantly, those supporting and supervising teachers of mathematics, can best be seen by comparison to teachers of other disciplines.

Here's how I see it: Over the past twenty years, teachers of language arts have been forced to replace one Shakespearean sonnet and one Dickens novel with a Maya Angelou poem and a novel like *Fahrenheit 451*. But genre is still genre, plot is still plot, and literature is taught as it was in high school, as it was in college, and as it was twenty years ago. Teachers of social studies have advanced over the same twenty years from the filmstrip projector to the 35mm projector to the VCR—while the Civil War and its causes haven't changed much. Compare this to teachers of mathematics who wrestle daily with what to do about long division, or how much time to spend on a skill that is no longer done with paper and pencil, or what to do about the "solve" button on a calculator that makes an agonizingly large proportion of the high school curriculum obsolete.

Although this comparison may suffer from a bit of hyperbole, the simple fact is that mathematics is different. The changes, the choices, and the decisions faced by teachers of mathematics are quantitatively different from those of teachers of other disciplines. We need to make the case that, given the differential needs, equality of professional development resources at this time is not equity, nor is it wise.

Obstacles to Change

Before examining a set of strategies to assist teachers and to scale up reform efforts, it is critical to pause and delineate the obstacles to change that the vast majority of teachers face daily.

Professional Isolation

It is unreasonable to expect teachers to implement changes on the order of what is needed when so much of their professional lives is conducted in such isolation. Teachers cannot be expected to implement the kinds of changes involving new technologies, new programs, and new approaches when they are unaware of available resources and instructional materials. Without support for ongoing professional development, opportunities to attend conferences, and access to professional journals, teachers and their supervisors remain unacceptably ignorant of the paths to change and improvement. It is inconceivable that we would be as complacent about the professional isolation of those in the medical profession. Yet the abiding sense that teachers arrive in a classroom on day one fully prepared to teach for thirty years with only minimal professional growth lingers dangerously in our culture.

Lack of Confidence and Fear of Change

It is also critical to remember that as educators, our first and foremost responsibility is to serve as perpetuators of the culture. We tend not to be radical agents of change. In fact, educators have been and continue to be hired to pass on the rich lore, traditions, and mores of the culture. And what more powerful elements of our mathematical culture exist than things like long division, the quadratic formula, and drill-and-kill worksheets? That is why changing the traditional curriculum and shifting time-honored instructional practices requires a degree of self-confidence and a willingness to take risks that the teaching profession has rarely reinforced.

Fear of Failure

Like in most of life, it is often much safer and much easier to maintain the mediocrity of the status quo than it is to risk the failure that change might entail. Teachers legitimately worry that they have failed when a principal criticizes an active, cooperatively grouped classroom as "too noisy" and "insufficiently under control." Teachers legitimately worry that they have failed when, after an exciting mathematical exploration with several engaging tangents, students say "This was fun. Do we have to do real math tomorrow?" or ask "When are we going to get to do math?"—having been conditioned to think that learning mathematics consists solely of individual practice of newly presented procedures. And teachers legitimately worry that they have failed when a colleague who now has several students whom they taught the previous year asks why they didn't teach a particular skill that was deemed to be obsolete and omitted to make room for a new unit on, for example, data analysis. No one likes to fail or to feel in jeopardy of failing. So it should not be surprising that teachers often structure their behavior to avoid any real deviation from tried-and-true methods. There is a strong tendency to "go along to get along" even when it is obvious that "going along" isn't meeting students' needs. Although "nothing ventured, nothing gained" is an apt aphorism for much of life, "nothing risked, nothing failed" is a far more powerful descriptor of what it too often done in schools.

Lack of Support

Given how scary and difficult it therefore is to make change, it should be obvious that support is crucial for people being asked to change. All who call for change must understand that without both moral and tangible support and ongoing encouragement from colleagues and administrators, few will take the requisite risks. Without support in the face of the misguided complaints of a few vocal parents, few teachers will change. Without support for quality professional development and time for sharing ideas and practices, little change is possible, and without the financial support for calculators, computers, and newer instructional materials, change is nearly impossible. Although beliefs and will are more important than money, without a reasonable financial investment—the most tangible form of support—little change is likely.

Insufficient Time

The blunt truth is that there is never enough time to do all we want to do. However, as individuals and groups of individuals, we have always displayed an uncanny ability to find time for what we valued and needed to do. Teachers, administrators, faculties, and mathematics departments will always use the excuse of insufficient time to make change. But when and where there is a will—a collegial commitment—to making change to better serve students, insufficient time no longer remains an insurmountable obstacle.

Overcoming the Obstacles

Given the ways in which teachers of mathematics are truly different and the magnitude of the obstacles they face, it is not surprising that reforming mathematics programs is such a Herculean task. However, the fact that pockets of excellence and reformed practices exist throughout the United States is testimony to the fact that it can be done. How? It can happen through equally Herculean efforts in the obstacle-overcoming arenas of professional development, professional sharing to reduce isolation, and leadership strategies that empower teachers. The antidotes of sharing, supporting, and risk-taking form the bedrock of enhanced professionalism and are the key tools that principals and other school leaders can use to overcome these obstacles.

Professional Development

The overarching construct for designing effective professional development for teachers of mathematics is that these developmental activities for teachers should parallel the effective instructional and assessment strategies we advocate in our standards for students. That is:

- Just as students need to be actively engaged in their own learning and construct their own understanding, so too must professional development for teachers actively engage them in the process of constructing understanding of mathematics, pedagogy, and students.

- Just as students need time to explore, practice, refine, and apply new understandings, so too must professional development for teachers provide adequate time and support to explore, practice, discuss, refine, apply, and reflect upon new ideas, techniques, and practices.

- Just as students need feedback and support from teachers and peers, so too do teachers need feedback and support from colleagues and supervisors, particularly when changes are being implemented.

- Just as classrooms are the primary unit of focus for students, so too must school and department faculties be the primary unit of attention when implementing effective professional development.

- Just as student learning of mathematics is the ultimate goal of classroom instruction, so too must student learning of mathematics be the ultimate goal of all professional development.

In other words, we must model in our practices that which we preach: what constitutes good instruction for our students is also what constitutes effective professional development for our colleagues. More specifically, we must adopt the following professional development practices:

Common Readings and Focused Discussions

"Communities of learners" are developed at group readings and discussion groups. Selected journal articles and passages from the NCTM Standards are excellent fodder for discussions that can be built around focus questions like:

- To what degree are we already addressing the issue or issues raised in this article?

- In what ways are we not addressing all or part of this issue?

- What are the reasons that we are not addressing this issue?

- What steps can we take to make improvements and narrow the gap between what we are currently doing and what we would like to do?

The articles included in the Appendix also provide excellent fodder for these focused discussions and help to engage people's beliefs and biases about mathematics instruction.

Demonstration Classes and Videotaped Lessons

Teachers have the opportunity to see and discuss what colleagues are doing by viewing videos of colleagues teaching or collaboratively watching a colleague teach. These activities foster a strong sense that "we're all in this together" and often provide a healthy, comic relief that strengthens a mathematics department or a grade-level team of teachers. In addition, videotapes and demonstration lessons provide invaluable insights into what is really going on in neighboring classrooms and communicate powerfully that teachers are not alone in what they face.

Faculty Seminars

Teachers can take control of their own professional growth by attending seminars. For some issues—particularly those relating to mathematical knowledge—readings, discussions, and viewing lessons are insufficient to raise the collective knowledge base of a group of teachers. For example, before plunging into graphics calculators or topics in discrete mathematics or algebraic thinking in elementary grades, teachers need to confront their own learning needs. Department and faculty seminars are excellent vehicles to meet such needs to know more mathematics or to learn about topics or techniques that were not offered or needed ten or twenty years ago. Such seminars, organized by and for colleagues and conducted by fellow teachers or outside resource people allow a department or a faculty to admit and address their needs. Just as a powerful camaraderie builds among students in a group that struggles together, so too do faculties build an esprit de corps through such seminars that makes learning a far less threatening experience.

Professional Sharing

One of the most serious obstacles to change and improvement is the professional isolation of most teachers. To reduce this debilitating isolation, we must make professional interaction and sharing the centerpiece of what we do. Whether by peer observations; team-teaching; formal and informal opportunities for professional sharing stimulated by common readings, common problems, or student work; issue-focused faculty or department meetings; action research teams; courses committees; or simply common planning time—it is time to help our colleagues become dynamic communities of learners, rather than just assortments of educators working in the same school or district. We know that professional interaction—often informal and unstructured—is often far more influential than more formally organized professional development. We act on this knowledge when we adopt practices that reduce isolation, such as those that follow.

Faculty and Department Meetings

Colleagues can come together to share, support, and learn at professionally enriching meetings. Such meetings should

- be conducted regularly, with notification made well in advance and with agendas published and distributed prior to the meeting;
- limit administrivia, including scheduling, inventory, ordering, grading, etc., to no more than 25 percent of the meeting;
- include reports from faculty or department members serving on school and department committees;

- systematically encourage sharing, questioning, and suggestions about issues of curriculum, instruction, and assessment;
- often include a "key topic of the meeting" featuring discussion led, on a rotating basis, by members of the faculty; and
- conclude with a summary of assignments for the next meeting.

Classroom Visits

In Japan, teachers are often found in the backs of classrooms observing colleagues. One of the easiest ways to reduce isolation and insulation is through school or department expectation that teachers regularly and informally visit the classrooms of their colleagues. Such periodic visits—made during preparation times at the middle and high school levels or when students are in art, music, or physical education at the elementary level—are often uncomfortable at first, but soon become standard operating procedure as teachers come to welcome and expect constructive feedback from colleagues. Sitting in each other's classrooms—even for as little as twenty minutes—often initiates some of the most useful collegial discussions and experimentation and makes risk-taking far more likely and far easier.

Grade-Level and Course Committees

Teachers assume ownership over what they teach when they take an active role in developing the curriculum and instructional approaches. In many effective mathematics programs, the critical responsibility for curricular and instructional updating is assigned to grade-level and course committees comprised of teachers who daily teach that course in that grade. Such committees, one for each grade level and major mathematics course, consist of several teachers who are charged with making annual recommendations to their colleagues regarding content additions and deletions, instructional practices and materials, and assessments—including course final exams or end-of-grade, criterion-referenced tests. Grade-level and course committees are effective vehicles for institutionalizing sharing and substantive collegial interaction, as well as excellent mechanisms for giving teachers ownership over the improvement of practice.

Leadership

What is obvious in education, and in all other settings, is that leadership remains the critical variable for change to occur and for change to be institutionalized in schools and districts. The three leadership strategies that I have found to be significant are granting permission, validating outliers, and catching the flak.

Granting Permission

Instead of telling people what to do, an alternative strategy is giving people permission to do what you would like them to do anyway. For example, in Connecticut, we've been using the revised objectives on our state tests in mathematics to give teachers permission to limit all paper-and-pencil multiplication to one-digit factors, arguing that two- and three-digit factors are fodder only for estimation, calculators, or both. We've given similar public permission to reduce the computational load to one-digit divisors in division and limit fractional computation to reasonable denominators (as opposed to sevenths and ninths).

Similarly, I am often struck by the degree of embarrassment expressed when teachers I've observed have made minor computational errors in the midst of lessons. Again, "permission to make a few mistakes," especially if technology or manipulative materials are being used, communicates that perfection is not expected and goes a long way to encourage and support risk-taking.

Leaders need to give colleagues permission to skip unnecessary lessons or even whole chapters in textbooks, permission to try new materials, permission to experiment with portfolios, permission to deviate, and permission to take risks.

Validating Outliers

Every one of us is blessed with exemplary colleagues. These are the teachers, administrators, and coworkers who are ahead of the curve. They are the people who are hard at work daily making the vision of the Standards a reality in their classes, schools, and districts. Everyone knows who these people are and we know they are the ones who make us look good. Unfortunately, within the culture of many schools, many of these people are outliers. They are often shunned by their colleagues, and they are uncertain the extra work they do and the risks they take are worth the extra time, effort, and grief. I believe that one of the critical aspects of our job is the systematic and ongoing validation of these special outliers.

As leaders, we need to encourage these people. We need to provide them with extra support and nurture them as a precious resource. We need to assure them that the eccentricity so often ascribed to them is a crucial and valued source of their professional competence. We need to reassure them that their time and efforts truly are appreciated. And we need to provide opportunities for networking and sharing among these atypical educators.

Catching the Flak

In these times of increasingly strident backlash and increasingly angry assaults on what we do, it's natural for people to become a little gun-shy. At exactly the point when the changes recommended by the mathematics reform effort require a little risk-taking, many of us encounter conditions that make it just that much harder to take these risks. Think of the wary parent taking it out on a teacher who listened to us and reduced the frequency of drill-and-practice worksheets. Or think of the frustrated guidance counselor taking it out on the teachers who listened to us and are trying to implement an algebra-for-all philosophy.

Leaders run flak intereference. They "catch the flak" and protect the people on the firing line by meeting with the disgruntled parents or by helping wayward guidance counselors understand the mathematics program. Leaders intercede when administrators prevent teachers from moving ahead, and they assure that the inevitable backlash is responded to head-on. In short, they assume responsibility and don't leave others holding the bag.

I mentioned earlier, "while 'nothing ventured, nothing gained' is an apt aphorism for much of life, 'nothing risked, nothing failed' is a far more powerful descriptor of what we do in schools." I believe this applies as much to leaders unwilling to take risks as it does to teachers unwilling to change.

7 Changing the System: How to Assure Quality*

Too often it appears that policy makers believe that changes like those advocated in this book can be mandated from above or implemented by fiat of some sort. Nothing is further from the truth or more likely to result in demoralization, frustration, and little real change. Researchers of school change and those who have successfully made improvements understand that teaching resides within a system and that changing teaching requires changes in the system. Frequently lost in the discussions about new standards for curriculum and about shifting instructional practices is the need for a set of *program delivery standards* that support curricular and instructional changes.

While working to implement systemic change in Connecticut, the following fifteen program components have emerged as a set of critical programmatic components that support a high-performance mathematics program. Although a strong program can certainly be implemented in the absence of one or more of these standards, attending to all of them significantly increases the chances that the transition to sensible, sense-making mathematics will be positive and productive. That is why each deserves careful thought and consideration by all principals and other school leaders. The fifteen components are:

1. Curriculum
2. Instructional Materials
3. Instructional Technology
4. Instructional Time

---

*Chapter 7 is an adaptation of Chapter 3 of *A Guide to K–12 Program Development in Mathematics*, copyright 1999 by the Connecticut State Board of Education. Adapted with permission.

5. Instructional Connections

6. Assessment of Students

7. Professional Interaction

8. Professional Development

9. Professional Supervision and Evaluation

10. Monitoring Programs

11. Tracking and Leveling

12. Remedial Assistance and Student Support

13. Articulation and Alignment

14. Resource Personnel and Leadership

15. Administrative Understanding and Support

This chapter presents each of these fifteen components with a statement of the standard and a brief elaboration that describes the key elements of a program that meets the standard. Any and all discussions and planning relating to the improvement of mathematics programs must attend to each of these components.

Curriculum

A high-quality mathematics program is defined, guided, and supported by a comprehensive, developmentally appropriate, written curriculum that is consistent with the vision of the NCTM standards and incorporates expectations of all valued assessment systems used to assess program effectiveness.

Too often, a district's curriculum guide gathers dust in a bottom drawer. Too often, summer curriculum committee work merely codifies the table of contents of the adopted textbook. And too often, teachers are given a series of conflicting messages to "follow the text," "follow the curriculum guide," and "get students ready for the test." These problems can be overcome when a mathematics program is driven by a comprehensive, teacher-friendly curriculum guide that provides clear direction, articulation between grades and successive courses, and coherence among the program's components.

A school or district's mathematics curriculum should delineate the overarching philosophy and goals of the program, present the key objectives or outcomes for each grade level or course, provide illustrative examples, tasks, and/or activities, indicate how the outcomes or objectives will be assessed, and list available resources for implementing the curriculum. In addition, a K–12 curriculum should assure smooth transition from grade to grade and course to course. In short, written curriculum guides should provide teachers and others with clear answers to the questions: "What exactly are my students expected to learn this year?" and "What skills, concepts, and understandings should I be held accountable for teaching this year?"

Instructional Materials

A high-quality mathematics program provides each student with, and makes effective use of, appropriate instructional print materials, as well as provides an adequate supply of nonprint materials to accomplish the goals of the curriculum.

Mathematics used to be the easiest of all major disciplines to support financially. Purchase one textbook for each student and an accompanying teacher's guide for each teacher, place some blank paper, lined paper, and graph paper in each classroom, ensure that each teacher has a blackboard and an ample supply of chalk, and maybe provide an overhead projector. These limited materials may have worked well to deliver a program limited to the mastery of arithmetic, but they are insufficient to support a high-quality mathematics curriculum.

In addition to a core text or, increasingly, a set of core modules, teachers need ready access to alternative textbooks, supplemental print materials, measuring devices, geometric models, and a host of grade-level or course-appropriate manipulative materials. In addition, teachers need access to an overhead projector to help present material visually and copying machines to quickly and efficiently reproduce diverse instructional materials and assessments that support the instructional program.

Without access to such an array of nontext materials, teachers' ability to deliver the kind of active instruction envisioned in this book is severely compromised.

Instructional Technology

A high-quality mathematics program ensures that each student has access to necessary technological tools and makes full use of calculators and computer software to implement the goals of the curriculum.

In every sector of our society, technology has changed how we do business, how we manufacture things, how we stay informed, and how we live our lives. Sadly, most schools lag far behind most other institutions when it comes to making full use of technology. The time has come for schools to enter the technological era and shift the fundamental delivery system of education in ways not seen since the invention of books and movable type in the fifteenth century.

Technology, particularly calculators that are now as commonplace as pencils, interactive probes that make algebra come alive, spreadsheets and graphing utilities that permeate the business world, and word-processing capability, must be available and incorporated into the K–12 mathematics program. Just as it is inconceivable to run a bank with the ledger cards of old, or a supermarket with the manual cash registers of yesterday, it is impossible to build a high-quality mathematics program with use of just paper and pencil.

Every teacher of mathematics must recognize that technology has made some mathematics entirely obsolete (e.g., calculating cube roots), some mathematics more readily accessible to students (e.g., exponential functions), and some mathematics possible for the first time (e.g., fractals). For this reason, an effective K–12 mathematics program is built on the assumptions that

- all students have access to appropriate calculators beginning no later than grade four;

- all teachers have overhead-projector-compatible calculators and LCD panels connected to a classroom demonstration computer; and

- all schools have site-licensed tool and utility software readily available for student and teacher use to enhance student learning of mathematics.

Instructional Time

A high-quality mathematics program provides time allocations for mathematics instruction of at least forty-five minutes per day at the primary level, at least sixty minutes per day at the intermediate level, and the equivalent of at least one forty-five-minute period per day at the middle school, junior high, and senior high school levels for formal mathematics instruction, supplemented less formally, through interdisciplinary activities and homework.

It is self-evident that time—formal allocations of minutes per day, informal and interdisciplinary minutes per week, and the overall quality of how the time is used—is a critical variable in assuring a high-quality program. Students whose formal mathematics period is sixty minutes per day receive nearly 180 hours of instruction a year, fully 50 percent more time than students in forty-minute periods. Moreover, students who complete twenty minutes of meaningful homework four nights per week spend over forty additional hours per school year engaged in mathematical tasks. Similarly, students in classes where the daily routine involves significant class time going over homework and starting on new homework receive far less productive instructional time than those in classes where students are actively involved exploring, investigating, and solving problems.

Thus, the 45- and 60-minute-per-day recommendations represent only *minimum* guidelines intended to ensure that schools schedule enough time for teachers and students to be reasonably able to meet the goals of the curriculum. It should be understood that the mathematics program must be richly supported by mathematics that is embedded in the science, social studies, and vocational educational curricula. It is also expected that these allocations are supplemented through interdisciplinary and integrated tasks and units and by the ongoing, everyday use of mathematics to solve school and classroom problems. In addition, nothing in this standard should preclude the scheduling of longer blocks of time to allow students to become more deeply involved in activities and projects.

Finally, at the high school level, consideration may be given to alternative scheduling that provides for longer class periods, fewer classes per day for both students and teachers, and fewer students per teacher per semester.

Instructional Connections

A high-quality mathematics program regularly makes connections both within mathematics and between mathematics and other subject areas so that students make and see the connections among the major mathematics curriculum strands and between mathematics and other disciplines.

For too long, for too many students, learning mathematics has meant moving from topic to topic, and from chapter to chapter, with little regard to the connections between and among these topics or chapters, and even less attention to the connections between the topics and their application in the world and in other disciplines. This lack of connection results in students being forced to learn and memorize far too many bits of information without benefit of generalizing principles or real-world contexts that make learning easier, more enjoyable, and more significant. A more inquiry-based approach tends to naturally support these instructional connections, and a more interdisciplinary approach tends to support enhanced exploration and inquiry.

One of the hallmarks of the NCTM standards is the emphasis on mathematical connections as one of the foci of all mathematics instruction. Rather than continue to view the mathematics curriculum as composed of several discrete strands—computation, measurement, geometry, algebra—that are often taught in isolation, a high-quality program regularly fosters connections between and among these strands as well as links the mathematics to everyday experiences and other disciplines.

Assessment of Students

A high-quality mathematics program has a coherent system of assessment that is closely aligned with the curricular and instructional goals of the program and that promotes the ongoing improvement of instruction.

In corporate America it is said that "what is inspected, is respected." Similarly, in schools, what is assessed and how it is assessed communicate most clearly what is valued. If the vision of a curriculum oriented to thinking, reasoning, and problem solving is to become a reality, our entire system of assessment and how we hold students accountable must shift. The traditional right/wrong forms of assessment may have been appropriate for assessing the success of a rule-driven, fact-oriented curriculum, but it is increasingly clear that such forms of testing are insufficient to support the curricular and instructional changes that are needed.

Accordingly, a high-quality mathematics program must incorporate more powerful assessments of demonstrated accomplishments, using observations, performances, projects, and/or portfolios. In fact, our entire system of accountability must shift from the relative standards of national percentiles and designations of percentages above and below remedial standards to more holistic judgments of student work, based on clear criteria for expected performance, that hold students accountable for meeting high standards. The need to make these newer and more sophisticated judgments is one of the reasons for significant increases in various types of performance assessment being advocated as better ways to measure student achievement.

When one defines assessment as a process of gathering evidence about a student's knowledge of, ability to use, and disposition toward, mathematics and of making inferences from that evidence for a variety of purposes, one begins to see assessment as the third interdependent component of a triangle: curriculum (what to teach), instruction (how to teach), and assessment (how well has learning occurred).

Professional Interaction

A high-quality mathematics program ensures that teachers have ample time and diverse mechanisms to interact professionally on substantive matters of curriculum, pedagogy, and assessment.

The professional isolation of teachers is frequently cited as the most serious impediment to improved curriculum, instruction, and assessment. Most teachers practice their craft behind closed doors, minimally aware of what their colleagues are doing, usually unobserved and under supported. Far too often, teachers' frames of reference are how they were taught, not how their colleagues are teaching. Common problems are too often solved individually rather than by seeking cooperative and collaborative solutions to shared concerns.

The magnitude of the change that teachers of mathematics are being asked to make requires far greater opportunities for substantive professional interaction. This interaction can and must take many forms. For example, teachers can engage in team-teaching and peer observations. Teachers can use videotapes of themselves or colleagues as discussion fodder, or they can conduct common planning through course committees (for example, the Algebra committee) or district-wide grade-level meetings. Principals and district administrators can rearrange schedules to provide common planning time so that teachers can work collaboratively and share ideas, experiences, and their collective wisdom of practice.

The professional interaction described in this standard envisions teachers as collaborative leaders, not as passive followers. It envisions teachers forming study groups, conducting informal research in their classes, and engaging in the inquiry that embodies lifelong learning.

Professional Development

A high-quality mathematics program is supported by a comprehensive program of professional development that focuses on issues of curriculum, pedagogy, and assessment, recognizes the importance of ongoing professional growth, and provides opportunities to participate in conferences, seminars, and institutes.

Once again, in light of the magnitude of the change that teachers of mathematics are being asked to make, it must be clearly understood that it is entirely unreasonable to expect teachers of mathematics to implement these changes in curriculum, instruction, and assessment when they are unaware of available programs, resources, and materials, and when there is so little time for reflection on these changes. Without planned, sustained, and ongoing professional development, including opportunities to attend conferences and seminars, access to professional journals, encouragement to visit with colleagues, and time for reflection, teachers too often remain unaware of the paths to change and improvement. In fact, many observers of Japanese schools cite the time allocated to just these forms of professional development and professional interaction as one of the starkest differences between the two systems.

For these reasons, an ongoing system of professional development for teachers of mathematics that is responsive to identified instructional needs, adequately funded, and supported with sufficient time, must be in place within every school and district. In addition to the professional interaction strategies previously described, professional development opportunities scheduled for after-school, weekends, and summer must be supplemented with school-day released time opportunities.

Professional Supervision and Evaluation

A high-quality mathematics program includes a system of professional supervision and evaluation that sets high standards of professional performance and is supported by programs and policies to assure that these standards are met.

Just as the methods and techniques of student assessment must change to account for measuring newer and broader outcomes, so too must methods and techniques of teacher evaluation change to account for different definitions of productivity and effectiveness. The commonplace practice of casual and infrequent classroom observation, often carried out in a perfunctory manner, insufficiently drives the improvement in practice and, thus, student achievement. Indeed, professional evaluation that supports a high-quality mathematics program needs to be broadened in scope and deepened in rigor. Administrators and supervisors must be better trained and must be more knowledgeable about effective mathematics curriculum and instruction. In addition, professional evaluation must go beyond periodic observations and include such activities as the development and peer review of professional performance portfolios and the analysis of student work and student achievement.

It is critical that classroom teachers receive constructive support—as they are supervised *and* as they are evaluated—so that excellence in teaching becomes a realistic and attainable goal for all.

Monitoring Programs

A high-quality mathematics program has a set of coordinated procedures that provide ongoing monitoring and periodic evaluation of the entire program to assure that student achievement goals are being met.

Every program in every school system should be periodically subjected to careful scrutiny. Those within the system, and increasingly, those outside the system have a right to definitive answers to questions such as:

- Is the program working for all students?
- Is the curriculum meeting the needs of students and the broader society?
- Is instruction provided in ways that maximize student achievement?
- Are students achieving in sufficient numbers and at high enough levels, and, if not, why?

- Are all necessary program components in place and aligned to achieve program goals?

To ensure a high-quality mathematics program, it is necessary to conduct periodic and comprehensive reviews of the entire program to answer these and other questions, publicly report findings, and implement changes on the basis of the review.

Tracking and Leveling

A high-quality mathematics program minimizes the leveling, sorting, and tracking of students while fully meeting the diverse and individual needs of all students.

No single component of the educational system more powerfully communicates the expectations—both high and low—we hold for young people than the ways in which schools sort, level, and track students. A major step in moving toward the vision of "mathematics for all" is a dramatic decrease in the ability-grouping, leveling, and tracking of students. This does not mean abandoning all ability groups; it does not mean the elimination of all honors courses; and it does not mean all students grouped heterogeneously all the time. It does mean, however, a change in policy at the school and district levels regarding ability-grouping and tracking so that no student is denied access to a rich and demanding mathematics program best suited to his or her individual needs and interests. In addition, such a policy recognizes that flexible grouping and collaborative teaching *can* be appropriate strategies for best meeting individual needs and helping to support inclusion practices.

Stated differently, it must be recognized that the current gap in breadth, depth, and rigor between what is provided for the top 20 percent and for the bottom 20 percent must be narrowed significantly by raising expectations for the bottom 20 percent. However, it must also be recognized that it is *not* reasonable that expectations for the top 20 percent be identical to those for the bottom 20 percent.

Remedial Assistance and Student Support

A high-quality mathematics program provides supplemental instructional services to assure that all students have the opportunity to meet the goals and expectations of the program.

Although individual and diverse backgrounds, interests, learning styles or preferences, and abilities are widely recognized, schools often overlook, and even ignore, these differences by keeping learning *time* a constant.

There are one-year courses, forty-minute classes, fifteen-minute quizzes, and two-minute fact drills that all students take. Common sense dictates that some students need less time and others need more time to be able to reasonably meet the goals for any lesson, unit, year, or program. One way that time becomes a variable used to better meet individual student needs is through the provision of extra, remedial, or compensatory instruction for those students for whom traditional time allocations are insufficient.

In addition to time adjustments, effective remedial and supplemental programs must also address adjustments in instructional methods and formats. For example, among the alternative ways that students can be better supported are via

- teachers who possess a wide repertoire of strategies, assorted instructional materials, including hands-on materials and high-quality software, and who supplement daily instruction for needy students;
- math centers that are well stocked with materials, supplemental resources, and computers, and that are staffed with trained and knowledgeable personnel;
- after-hours programs such as after-school clinics, Saturday academies, and summer enrichment programs; and
- support personnel available to work with students within classrooms rather than in pull-out situations and who work closely with regular classroom teachers.

Articulation and Alignment

A high-quality mathematics program evolves coherently, grade-by-grade and course-by-course, from kindergarten through twelfth grade and displays an alignment of curriculum, instructional materials, professional development, and assessment that are all implemented to attain the overarching goals of the program.

Two often noted characteristics of what has been referred to as the "underachieving mathematics curriculum" are the mixed, and often conflicting, messages given to teachers about what should be taught, how it should be taught, and how it will be assessed on the one hand, and the lack of a smooth flow of mathematical content as students progress from kindergarten through twelfth grade on the other hand.

To eliminate these unwanted features, curriculum guides must replace textbooks and tests as the primary driver of the program. In addition to delineating content expectations, these curriculum guides need to provide both instructional suggestions and assessment possibilities to ensure tighter alignment. Similarly, curriculum guides must be designed to ensure a developmentally appropriate sequence of outcomes, recognizing the need for exploratory exposure to mathematical ideas, opportunities to master these ideas, and time to review and reinforce these ideas. In addition, middle and high school course offerings must likewise be an articulated sequence that maximizes student readiness for each succeeding course. A common vehicle for increasing the articulation and coordination of the curriculum is through grade-level meetings of two consecutive grades and meetings of course committees where teachers share problems and concerns and make necessary adjustments.

Resource Personnel and Leadership

A high-quality mathematics program assigns the responsibility for the ongoing implementation and improvement of the program to qualified coordinators, supervisors, resource personnel, and/or department chairpeople in order to provide support, coordination, supervision, and leadership.

Each of the previously discussed components make it increasingly clear that a high-quality K–12 mathematics program entails a complex web of ongoing activity, change, and support. Such a program cannot just be put in place and expected to run by itself for some period of time. In fact, like every other aspect of a school system, the effectiveness and vitality of a district's K–12 mathematics program depends critically on the assignment of responsibility for program oversight and coordination to one or more individuals. All too often when program leadership and responsibility for ongoing implementation and improvement are not vested in one or more individuals, the focus on program quality and improvement tends to fall through the cracks and fragment under the weight of other priorities.

Thus, given that high-quality programs require that a vision of reform be created and nurtured, that teachers be kept abreast of changes and aware of professional development opportunities, and that curricular, instructional, and assessment improvement are ongoing processes, it is imperative that leadership of and responsibility for the mathematics program be assigned and maintained at all levels.

Administrative Understanding and Support

A high-quality mathematics program receives strong support from principals and central office administrators to ensure that these standards are met.

These program delivery standards do not get implemented automatically or because they are listed and described in a curriculum guide. Rather, their implementation requires the understanding and tangible support of principals, curriculum coordinators, assistant superintendents, and superintendents. Although implementation of a curriculum and effective delivery of instruction occurs in thousands of classrooms, the critical support for teachers and understanding of the program described in this chapter derive from the beliefs and actions of hundreds of school and district administrators.

These administrators are key for setting a tone for continuous review and improvement, for maintaining continually higher expectations, and for providing teachers with the financial, material, and professional development support they need to meet the school or district's objectives. Effective administrators strengthen a mathematics program by encouraging experimentation, by facilitating the review and use of school and district assessment data, and by keeping concern for student achievement in mathematics on the front burner at all times. Effective administrators also "grant permission" for teachers to take risks and shift both curriculum and instruction. In addition, administrators play a key role in encouraging and supporting teachers who are struggling to change old habits and adopt new practices.

Conclusion

Passing Along Lessons Learned

For the past twenty-one years, I have been blessed. As a mathematics consultant in the Connecticut Department of Education, I have had the opportunity to work in dozens of school districts, hundreds of schools, and with thousands of dedicated and professional teachers of mathematics. I have had the opportunity to work in an incredibly supportive and collegial state department of education where the question "How can we help?" has never been empty rhetoric. And I have had a wealth of varied experiences across the country as part of my activities within the National Council of Teachers of Mathematics and the National Council of Supervisors of Mathematics. Over this period of time and in these various roles, I have seen people make extraordinary changes. I have seen schools undergo major transformations and districts provide truly excellent mathematics programs. But far more often, I have watched as ignorance, confusion, fear, a lack of leadership, or simply an unwillingness to move has relegated children and young adults to a truly mind-numbing mathematics program. Through all this—some truly amazing, some good, some bad, and some downright ugly—I have learned immensely. Here is some of what I've learned and what I'd like to pass along to all who toil in the honorable vineyards of making mathematics truly work for all.

First, never stray from a *dogged focus on classroom instruction*. Just as Bill Clinton won in 1992 in part by making "It's the economy, stupid!" a campaign mantra, for educators and educational policy makers at all levels, the appropriate mantra must be "It's the classroom, stupid!" When all is said and done, it's not the buses, nor the buildings, nor the budgets that determine how much and how well students learn, it's the daily interactions between teachers and students, and among students, in the classrooms of every school that determine how much and how well students will learn. New materials, professional development, and effective supervision are all important only to the degree they support high-quality instructional interactions. When things are going well and students are learning, the causal path leads directly back to the classroom. Similarly, when things are not going well, when results are mediocre at best, and when students are bored and acting out, the same causal path points to the classroom. If one seeks to improve the quality of education and the quantity of student achievement, enhancing, empowering, energizing, and engaging teaching and teachers has always been and will continue to be the method of choice.

Second, I have come to believe that *assessment is the most powerful change lever in our arsenal.* Good tests nudge along improvements and push people to make change. Bad tests perpetuate mediocrity and reinforce counterproductive practices. In the daily lives of most teachers and students, it is the assessments that are used that communicate what we value. Think how often students ask "Is this going to be on the test?" When told "Yes," pencils and notebooks start to stir and attention gets paid. When told "No, this is just enrichment," eyes start to glaze over and heads start to nod off. That's why improving and better aligning high-stakes state assessments has been one of the most popular strategies for encouraging change. And that's why building influential and respected grade-level, criterion-referenced tests and common course final examinations are often more important than the curriculum upon which they are based. Anyone interested in what is valued in the intended curriculum needs look no further than the tests that students are given. When these tests regularly include interesting problems, extended tasks, explanations of reasoning, and justifications for actions and solutions, one can be sure reform is being supported and encouraged, and that the learning of important mathematics is being stressed.

Third, as I have tried to exemplify throughout this book, *everything we advocate must be grounded in concrete examples.* All good instruction is enhanced by examples that help the learner build on prior experiences, connect new ideas, concretize new concepts, and apply what is being learned. The same must be true in all our discussions about shifting mathematics programs. Unfortunately, as educators, we too often fall back upon the words of lectures and the abstractions of concepts, forgetting to consistently link our words and abstractions to what can actually be illustrated. That's why we must pause and show each other exactly what we mean with clear and compelling examples. And that's why exemplars, models, samples of student work, and videos are indispensable tools for helping people to understand our ideas and visualize our vision.

Fourth, we need to *toot our own horns* much more frequently and much more loudly that we are often comfortable doing. There is so much that is good in America's elementary, middle, and high schools. There is much mathematics learning that is working well for millions of students. And there are thousands of pockets of extraordinary accomplishments occurring daily in America's classrooms. But one would hardly know these things in the face of an incessant onslaught of news about the problems, the woes, and the failures of our schools. In far too many cases, we educators are our own worst enemies: at best, we think it's unprofessional and unbecoming to tout our successes, and at worst, we express our frustrations in public and reinforce the ever-present negative perceptions. The best solution is to become our own public relations officers. At all levels of the system, it is time to gather data on what is working, celebrate successes with great fanfare, and publicize our not inconsiderable accomplishments. All corporations have public information personnel who are assigned to churn out the good news and put the best possible spin on events. Every politician either has a press secretary or acts as his or her own press secretary to inform, promote, and publicize. Every school and every district should engage in commensurate promotion of the positive.

Finally, each of us must remember *how much difference one person can make*. The enduring, yet haunting, beauty of the education profession is that each and every educator has the potential to make an extraordinary difference in the lives of students. But it is usually years before that difference is recognized and rarely then is it even acknowledged. More often recognized, but no more frequently acknowledged, is the extraordinary difference every educator can make in the lives of colleagues. Thus, in classrooms and faculty rooms, in school, district, and state agency offices, the motivating force that makes educators so special is the understanding that taking the extra minute, going the extra mile, reaching out one additional time can, and often does, make the critical difference. Recognizing and acting on this simple truth can, and does, allow each of us to touch eternity.

Appendix: Discussion Starters

The eight articles provided in this appendix represent a diverse set of discussion stimuli to foster reflection about teaching and reforming school mathematics. They are all pieces I have written that for one reason or another have stirred up some degree of controversy. This controversy leads me to believe that each piece can serve as a strong catalyst for collegial discussion about the issues raised in this book and the issues that teachers encounter when they begin to adapt change. Accordingly, each piece can be used to help implement some of the strategies for overcoming obstacles suggested in Chapter 6.

It's Time to Abandon Computational Drudgery (But Not the Computation)

It's time to recognize that, for many students, real mathematical power, on the one hand, and facility with long paper-and-pencil computational procedures, on the other, are mutually exclusive. In fact, it's time to acknowledge that continuing to teach these increasingly obsolete skills to our students is not only unnecessary, but counterproductive and downright dangerous!

My intent in so brashly taking on one of the lingering pillars of basic elementary education is neither to be unduly confrontational nor impishly irresponsible. I am not seeking to wrap myself in the banner of radical reformers, nor to stir up the fundamentalists. Rather, my purpose is to raise an issue that is not going to disappear. It's an issue that must be discussed openly and honestly, and then resolved swiftly and clearly if we are to realize our aspirations for truly world-class schools.

First let's clarify exactly what is being proposed. This is *not* about reducing emphasis on one-digit addition, subtraction, multiplication, and division facts. These facts and the self-confidence that comes with their mastery are more important than ever. Nor is this about abandoning computation, which remains an indispensable part of the mathematics program, so long as it is done mentally, with a calculator, or via estimation. It *is* about the formal, paper-and-pencil computational procedures that constitute the core grade school mathematical experiences of most American youngsters. It's about mindless procedures like "carrying 3s into the 10s column," "6 times 7 is 42, put down 2 and carry the 4," and "8 from 2, can't do, cross out the 5, make it a 4, and borrow 10." It's also about memorized rules like "Yours is not to reason why, just invert and multiply" that, for most students, meaninglessly enter one ear and leave the other.

Usually, this is all it takes to start an avalanche of dismay. The most common reactions are: "But weren't those rules and procedures good enough for us?" "Isn't this just the 'new math' all over again?" "But what if the calculator is lost or the batteries die?" and "What about the basics?"

So let's make the case. Let's begin with what we know and what most of us can agree upon. Then let's see how acting on these agreements leads naturally and logically to abandoning computational drudgery.

We know that less than a generation ago, real people in real situations regularly put pencil to paper, used a little-understood procedure that had been practiced to the point of automaticity, and computed a solution to a problem involving numbers. Without the rote ability to perform the procedure, the needed solution was usually unattainable. We know with equal clarity that this is no longer how the real world works. All around us, real people in real situations regularly put finger to button and make critical decisions about which buttons to press, not where and how to carry threes into hundreds columns. We understand that this change is on the order of magnitude of the outhouse to indoor plumbing in terms of comfort and convenience, and of the sundial to digital timepieces in terms of accuracy and accessibility.

We also know that a curriculum dominated by a strict hierarchy of skills and procedures has meshed perfectly with the historically perceived mission that schools serve as society's primary sorting mechanism. What better vehicle for anointing the few and casting out the many than demanding mastery of increasingly complex computational procedures—most often taught and learned in mindless, rote fashion? And how else can we account for the obeisance paid to the bell curve of student achievement that results from norm-referenced standardized tests? But what is increasingly clear is how radically society's needs and expectations for schools have shifted. No longer are schools expected to serve as social and economic sorting machines. Instead, schools must become empowering machines. No longer simply perpetuators of the bell curve, where only some survive and even fewer truly thrive, schools and their mathematics programs must instill understanding and confidence in all. In short, we now understand that teaching formal rules for adding and subtracting decimals, like their "gone-and-not-missed" cousin, the square root algorithm, remains a vestige of a sort-em-out approach that continues to fail both kids and the society that so desperately needs a far more mathematically powerful citizenry.

We also know that we must differentiate the proverbial "baby" from the "bath water." The "baby" is having a $10 bill and seeing that Big Macs are $1.59 each. It's formulating questions about change and taxes, and it's figuring out how many could be bought. The core of mathematical power is explaining why you think six Big Macs is a reasonable estimate and why division is an appropriate operation in this situation. It's interpreting the 6.2893082 on the calculator display, or it's presenting alternative approaches using repetitive addition, repetitive subtraction, or trial and error with the multiplication key. Meanwhile, the "bath water" is a paper-and-pencil procedure for dividing 10 by 1.59 on which no sane person relies.

We know that it's time to change the "bath water" lest the "baby" continue to drown.

But none of this is as compelling as what we know about the sense of failure and the pain unnecessarily imposed on hundreds of thousands of students in the name of mastering these obsolete procedures. We know that many students are bored to death and frustrated to tears when faced with completing "exercises #1–29 (odd) on page 253." Compare the energy and enthusiasm of a class cooperatively learning statistics with bags of M&Ms to a class mindlessly and individually inverting and multiplying meaningless fractions to arrive at equally meaningless answers. Compare a class where students are estimating costs for a shopping spree from newspaper fliers prior to using calculators to see who comes closest to $100 to a class tediously finding sums of columns of numbers with no connection to the children's lives.

A few short years ago we had few or no alternatives to paper-and-pencil computation. A few short years ago we could even justify the pain and frustration we witnessed in our classes as necessary parts of learning what were then important skills. Today there are alternatives and there is no honest way to justify the psychic toll it takes. We need to admit that computational drill and practice devours an incredibly large proportion of instructional time, precluding any real chance for actually applying mathematics and developing the conceptual understanding that underlies mathematical literacy.

So why do we continue to impose these skills on our students and teachers? Because despite all the powerful reasons for change, schools are equally powerful perpetuators of what they've always done. Ask an educator why long division is still taught and one will hear that it's in the text, on the test, part of the curriculum, and/or always been taught. Never does one hear that it's needed or that it's important.

If we are true to our professed goals, the course is clear. It's time to build mathematics programs that engage and empower, unencumbered by the discriminatory shackles of computational drudgery. It's time to banish these vestiges of yesteryear from our schools and from our tests.

Adapted from "It's Time to Abandon Computational Algorithms," *Education Week*, February 9, 1994.

Four Teacher-Friendly Postulates
for Thriving in a Sea of Change

Many of us went into mathematics teaching because it was always so neat and clean. We felt an affinity toward teaching and learning mathematics because it was orderly and logical. There was almost always only one numerical answer arrived at by using one right procedure that could be easily graded as either right or wrong. We knew that with our beloved mathematics we suffered none of the gray areas that plague the disciplines of language arts and social studies. And we knew that we would be rewarded for teaching mathematics just as we ourselves were taught. But, oh, how things have changed!

Let's face it: the NCTM standards (1989, 1991) have made our professional lives much more challenging. Given how much the teaching of mathematics must change to serve a digitized world of calculators and computers and given the breadth of the recommendations of the standards, it's not surprising that many teachers of mathematics are frustrated and feel thoroughly challenged. To ease this inevitable frustration, I offer four perspective-building postulates for thriving in a sea of change.

Postulate 1: We are being asked to teach in distinctly different ways from how we were taught.

It is a long-accepted truth that most people parent as they were parented and most teachers teach as they were taught. We build on what is familiar because the familiar "feels right." However, to teach concepts, not just skills; to rely on cooperative groups; to work collaboratively with colleagues; and to assume the availability of calculators, are all parts of a very unfamiliar terrain for many of us. Neither previous generations of mathematics teachers, nor our colleagues in other disciplines, have had to face such a chasm between how they were taught and how they are being asked to teach. No wonder many of us are feeling disoriented and inadequate (see Postulate 4).

Because people can't do what people haven't seen or experienced, we need to create tangible and accessible models of curricular and instructional reform. We need to increase opportunities for collegial classroom visits, and we need to increase our reliance on videotapes of what the distinctly different forms of pedagogy look like.

Postulate 2: The traditional curriculum was designed to meet societal needs that no longer exist.

The bedrock upon which this entire reform movement rests is a clear understanding that society's needs and expectations for schools have shifted radically. No longer are schools expected to serve as society's primary sorting mechanisms. Instead, schools must become empowering machines. From schools as perpetuators of the bell curve, where only *some* were expected to survive and *even fewer* truly thrived, education must be a springboard where *all* must attain higher levels. This is why behaviors and attitudes that were rewarded a short decade or two ago now are under such scrutiny.

In the face of such emotionally trying bombardments, two very different responses to the standards and other aspects of the reform movement have become common. Some have basically ignored the entire movement, believing that "this too will pass." Others understand that change is required, but, sensing that they themselves are not really moving fast enough, begin to feel guilty about not doing more sooner. Denial and guilt are both entirely appropriate responses to the magnitude of the change swirling around us. However, neither response is particularly comforting, and neither represents the level of professionalism we expect from ourselves.

For comfort and a professional safety net, I find it helpful to remember that ignoring the need for change in mathematics ignores how radically different society's expectations for schools have become. And feeling guilty about what we've done in the past or about not changing fast enough ignores how effectively schools once met a set of needs that simply no longer exists.

Postulate 3: It is unreasonable to ask a professional to change much more than 10 percent a year, but it is unprofessional to change by much less than 10 percent a year.

It easily could be argued that the most disorienting element of our lives is the rate at which things are changing. Many have written about people's ability to accommodate to the ever increasing rate of change. In somewhat arbitrary, but certainly comforting, fashion, I have come to believe that something around 10 percent a year is a reasonable rate to expect. It's large enough to represent real and significant change, but small enough to be manageable.

One way to visualize change at this rate is to think about substituting one new unit into the year, shifting four weeks of instruction to address something new, or doing something in a very different way, e.g., changing questioning techniques or using journals. Using this incremental approach results in a change of nearly half of what we do in five years. Even the most radical proponent of reform should be satisfied with change of this magnitude in our mathematics classes, and even the most cautious and tradition-bound among us should be able to retain a real sense of control over such a rate of change.

Postulate 4: If you don't feel inadequate, you're probably not doing the job.

Just think what we are asking each other to do: increase the use of technology; use manipulatives and pictures with far greater frequency; make regular use of group work; focus on problems, communication, applications, and interdisciplinary approaches; teach far more heterogeneous groups; increase attention to statistics, geometry, and discrete mathematics; assess students in far more authentic and complex ways; and do it all yesterday and in ways that boost achievement overnight! Feeling overwhelmed by this torrent of change isn't weakness or unprofessional—it's an entirely rational response.

It should be obvious that no one can do it all. Just as no one expects a physician to be an expert in all aspects of medicine, it is just as unreasonable to expect a mathematics teacher in the 1990s to be an expert in all aspects of teaching mathematics. We must select a few areas of focus and balance the fears and worries we understandably have in some areas with the pride of accomplishment and success we find in other areas. We must accept the inevitability of a sense of inadequacy and use it to stimulate the ongoing growth and learning that characterizes the true professional. Only then will we be sufficiently armed, intellectually and emotionally, to thrive in the exhilarating, exhausting, and often overwhelming sea of change.

This article first appeared in *Mathematics Teacher*, September, 1994, National Council of Teachers of Mathematics.

Mathematics Program Leaders in Elementary, Middle, and High Schools

The National Council of Teachers of Mathematics believes that the designation and support of school and district-level mathematics program leaders are essential to the improvement of mathematics instruction and achievement for all students. These designated leaders should be responsible for coordinating the planning, implementation, and evaluation of mathematics programs. They should serve as informed resources in the areas of curriculum design, professional development, instructional strategies, student and program assessment, and the development of partnerships with the broader community.

In addition, NCTM believes that school and district-level mathematics program leaders are an indispensable component of providing high-quality mathematics programs for students and should be expected to

- address concerns and promote excellence in mathematics education for all students;
- be visionary agents of positive change, knowledgeable about national standards, aware of current research, and able to translate these standards and this research into classroom practice; and
- link stakeholders in education and enlist their support in improving the quality of the teaching and learning of mathematics.

It is clear that the demands upon teachers of mathematics have never been greater. Several trends stand out in particular:

- Society in general and a changing workplace demand broader mathematical literacy for every student.
- Technology forces reconsideration of what mathematics is essential and how best to teach this mathematics.

- National standards and the higher expectations they represent have heightened the need for updating the knowledge and skills of teachers of mathematics as these standards are translated into the district, school, and classroom levels.

NCTM believes that these demands, and the changes in classroom practice that they imply, require different and more effective forms of leadership to help shape and direct improvement. More specifically, NCTM believes the following list of responsibilities should be carried out by school and district-level mathematics program leaders.

Curriculum Design

- Coordinate the development and implementation of a sound and coherent K–12 mathematics curriculum.
- Ensure curricular alignment and coordination between grades, levels, and courses—including assisting teachers to understand the curriculum as a whole and their part of it.
- Assist teachers in using rich and challenging problems and activities that integrate mathematics into other disciplines and the content of other disciplines into mathematics.
- Guide the ongoing review and revision of the curriculum and ensure alignment with state and local guidelines.

Instructional Strategies and Materials

- Recommend programs and materials, and oversee their piloting, adoption, and the evaluation of their effectiveness.
- Consult with and acquaint teachers with successful and innovative strategies, including translating research findings into practice.
- Assist teachers in effectively using technology in daily instruction.
- Assist teachers by modeling effective instructional strategies.
- Work with teachers to encourage reflection and discussion of what is working, what is not working, and how to make improvements.

Assessment

- Assist teachers in designing and implementing a broad range of assessment tools.
- Ensure the alignment of assessment instruments with the curriculum.

- Collect and analyze data about what is and is not working, and use this data, including student assessment results, to improve curriculum and instruction.
- Interpret the results of assessment for parents and the community at large.

Professional Development

- Collaborate with the staff to determine needs and priorities for professional development.
- Conduct or facilitate professional development activities, and motivate colleagues to engage in ongoing professional growth and development.
- Encourage involvement in professional organizations.
- Design, encourage, and facilitate opportunities for professional sharing and interaction between and among colleagues, and advance other strategies that enhance professional communication.
- Promote mentoring of colleagues and professional visits among teachers.

Forging Partnerships

- Communicate with committees, school boards, administrators, teachers, parents, and students about the importance of mathematics and the need for high-quality mathematics programs.
- Cultivate connections with the postsecondary mathematics and mathematics education communities, and with local business and industry personnel.
- Establish and support forums and encourage dialogue among groups that influence the shape and direction of school mathematics programs.

Adapted from "Improving Student Achievement Through Designated District and School Mathematics Program Leaders," a position statement of the National Council of Supervisors of Mathematics, 1997.

Changing the System: Tidy Events and Messy Processes

I find it interesting that the more often we invoke the mantra "Change is a process, not an event," the more we seem to honor events as primary indicators of change.

Just think of how we answer the question "What's new?" We talk about our new curriculum or our new textbook. We speak about our new three-year mathematics graduation requirement—including algebra—or our new block schedule. We respond that we've got two new classroom sets of TI-83 calculators or that we've just finished a two-week summer workshop on the effective use of manipulatives. These are all obviously worthy of pride, but they all also tend to represent top-down, product-oriented, voted-in *events* that have only marginal impact on the overall system and that rarely result in substantive improvement.

Now think of how rarely "What's new?" is greeted by the far fuzzier—but far more influential—changes in process. For example, we hail the new materials we've adopted, but rarely acclaim the revisions to the materials-selection process that are more important than ever. We recognize staff development events, but rarely focus on the long-term process of educating principals, superintendents, and members of boards of education who are so crucial for the success of mathematics reform. And we still focus enormous time and energy on producing curriculum guides and frameworks that few bother to read, let alone use, when devoting a fraction of this time to assuring that our assessments were aligned with the curriculum would pay far richer systemic dividends.

But none of this should be surprising. It's easy to mandate such things as time requirements, curriculum guidelines, professional development sessions, and new materials. That is, it is easy to create an infrastructure from the top-down. It's an entirely different matter getting the infrastructure to work and changing beliefs, behaviors, and practices. This is where we need to facilitate, where we need processes, where change is bottom-up, and where our collective attention needs to be focused.

Accordingly, we must shift our thinking from the tidy planning and implementation of events to the messy establishment of ongoing processes that reform the system. We need to ask ourselves questions such as:

- What ongoing processes do we have in place to shift beliefs about mathematics and teaching mathematics?

- What ongoing processes do we have in place to significantly increase professional interaction?

- What ongoing processes do we have in place to enlist the active support of principals, superintendents, and members of boards of education?

- What ongoing processes do we have in place to engender stronger public support for high-quality mathematics education?

Nowhere in all the volumes of data and commentary on the recently released Third International Mathematics and Science Study (TIMSS) has this notion of a need to shift our attention from creating an infrastructure to *making the infrastructure work* been clearer than in the comparison of pedagogical approaches used in Germany, Japan, and the United States. After making a rather compelling case that the similarities in terms of curriculum, time, teachers, and students are far greater than the differences, TIMSS (*Pursuing Excellence*, pp. 42–44) presents stark differences in terms of typical eighth grade mathematics lessons. While the typical Japanese lesson parallels the vision of our standards and focuses on understanding, the typical United States lesson emphasizes skill acquisition (see Figure 3-6, page 31). The extensive videotape study also found that while over three-quarters of the grade eight topics were developed conceptually in Germany and Japan, only one-quarter of these topics were developed conceptually in the United States. Alternatively, over three-quarters of the topics taught in the United States were presented in the relatively passive, "teachers prescribe, students transcribe," mode with little attention to conceptual understanding (see Figure A-1).

What should be clear is that changing these classroom practices requires much more than the top-down events that merely build an infrastructure. Thanks to TIMSS, we know better than ever what problems we face. Thanks to the growing body of research on systemic reform, we have better answers than ever to solving these problems. All that's left is rolling up our sleeves and implementing the messy and varied processes that foster genuine systemic reform and improved student achievement. It's a challenge I believe we are up to.

This article first appeared in the January, 1997, *NCSM Newsletter*.

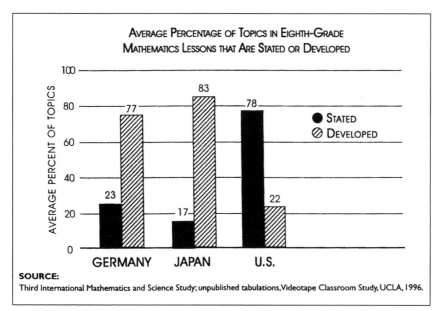

Figure A-1 Average percentage of topics in eighth grade mathematics lessons that are stated or developed

It's Still the Test, Stupid!

In our business, it's not the economy, "it's the test, stupid!" Let's face it—assessment is still the critical variable supporting or hindering reform. Unfortunately, district and state assessments appear to retard change far more often than they help to accelerate it. The truism is truer than ever: What we test and how we test it drives what we teach and how we teach it.

Hardly a workshop goes by without the all too common question: "I agree with everything you're saying, but what about the tests?" A question that is a stark reminder that

- when the tests we use—or are forced to use—don't allow students to use calculators, teacher are far less likely to integrate calculators into day-to-day instruction;

- when the tests continue to expect and report competency in multi-digit, paper-and-pencil computation, you can be sure that the 1990s curriculum doesn't look very different from the 1950s curriculum;

- when the tests continue to be limited to multiple-choice questions, most instruction will be limited to practice with isolated skills and procedures to get right answers; and

- when norm-referenced, standardized tests continue to be the primary accountability mechanism, complete with the pressure of front-page rankings of schools and districts, it's highly unlikely that the vision of the standards can take root and grow.

That's why the new Assessment Standards are so important to read, to share, to discuss, and to implement. And that's why the latest NCSM Source Book for Leaders entitled *Great Tasks and More: Camera Ready Resources on Mathematics Assessment* has been produced. I believe that this latest Source Book can serve as an instantaneous workshop-delivery kit or be used as a handbook for conducting demonstration classes. You will see that in addition to over 100 released assessment tasks, the Source Book also includes camera-ready copies of the NCTM Assessment Standards Speaker's Kit Masters, sample scoring rubrics, and several important articles to read and share.

We need to rededicate ourselves—at both the district and state levels—to assuring that our mandated accountability tests are aligned *with*, not antithetical to, the visions of important mathematics, communication, reasoning, and problem solving.

We need to work together—armed with our Assessment Standards and our Source Book to

- increase significantly the proportion of open-ended, constructed response items on all of our tests;
- assure that calculators are permitted and available for nearly all assessments and that any calculator is acceptable; and
- reduce significantly, especially now that Title I regulations have been changed, the reliance on multiple-choice, standardized tests!

Consider beginning today with a collegial discussion of the student work that arises from one of the tasks in the Source Book. Consider engaging parents or your board of education with such a task at their next meeting. Consider school-based discussions about the implications of each of the first six assessment standards and the degree to which they are reflected in the policies and practices in place in your school. Good luck and keep pushing!

This article first appeared in the March, 1996, *NCSM Newsletter*.

Giving Students the Benefit of the Doubt

It used to be so much easier. Doing mathematics meant getting right answers. Whether it was a straightforward exercise or a more involved problem, the choice was almost always between right and wrong—between a black check and a red "X". If right: Great! Full credit. If wrong: Tough! No credit. Correctness and accuracy were all that counted and grades were easily computed by aggregating the checks or subtracting the Xs from 100. Mathematics was the paragon of objectivity, and we rarely had to worry about giving students the benefit of the doubt because in the dichotomous world of right and wrong, there was simply no doubt.

But then came the expanded focus on solving problems and communicating mathematically. Along came accessible and inexpensive calculators that provided speed as well as accuracy. And with these changes we've had to deal with a growing recognition that authentic work and the demonstration of understanding was increasingly even more important than a page of right answers.

Very quickly these changes have made things very messy. We've been forced to enter the world of partial credit, holistic scoring, and rubrics. We've had to shift toward more subjective scoring schemas. And we've come to recognize the need to more frequently give our students the benefit of the doubt.

These issues recently became much clearer to me when we holistically scored the open-ended items on the tenth grade Connecticut Academic Performance Test (CAPT). We established a general policy that judgment calls were nearly always resolved by pausing and thinking about which score gave the student the benefit of the doubt. That is, did the response show sufficient evidence of understanding, even if the correct answer was missing?

We built the scoring system around the following four-point generic rubric or scoring guide:

1. A score of three reflects **full and complete** understanding of all concepts and processes embodied in the problem. It means that the task was addressed in a mathematically sound manner and that the response may contain minor arithmetic errors

2. A score of two reflects **reasonable**, although incomplete, understanding of the essential concepts and processes embodied in the problem. It means that the response contains most of the attributes of an appropriate response, however the flaws it contains do not offset countervailing evidence that the student understands the essential mathematical ideas addressed by the task.

3. A score of one reflects **limited** understanding of some of the concepts and processes embodied in the problem. It means that the response contains only some of the attributes of an appropriate response and that the flaws it contains provide evidence of insufficient understanding and knowledge of the ideas addressed by the task.

4. A score of zero reflects **merely an acquaintance** with the topic. It means that the response contains few or none of the attributes of an appropriate response and that there is little or no evidence of understanding of the ideas addressed by the task.

Our hope is that the use of this generic rubric on the CAPT test will encourage its widespread use on a much larger scale in classrooms across the state. Our hope is that educators will experiment with such four-point scoring scales as they move away from the traditional—albeit limiting—100-point scale with which we are so familiar. And our hope is that parents and students will come to appreciate that a three out of four holistic score tied to clearly articulated rubrics and samples of student work is a much more meaningful measure of accomplishment than a grade of 80 on an always changing scale of 100.

So welcome to the exciting world of increased ambiguity, more subjectivity, and harder-to-make judgments that characterize assessments of mathematical power. It sure used to be a lot easier, but that was when life was a lot simpler and mathematics was a lot narrower.

This article first appeared in the *ATOMIC Journal*, Spring 1995.

Beliefs: The Bedrock Upon Which Change is Built

The key to implementing the wide-ranging recommendations of the National Council of Teachers of Mathematics *Curriculum and Evaluation Standards* is our willingness and our ability to change. And the key to making change is changing our beliefs: our beliefs about mathematics, our beliefs about effective instruction, and our beliefs about our students.

1. Many still believe that mathematics is primarily adding, subtracting, multiplying, and dividing whole numbers, fractions, and decimals; that is, paper-and-pencil manipulation of numbers and symbols. Effective teachers increasingly believe that in a world of calculators and computers, mathematics is problem solving and reasoning; that is, applying mathematical concepts and skills to everyday and real-world situations.

2. Many still believe that mathematical achievement is best determined on the basis of proficiency in arithmetic and algebra. Effective teachers increasingly believe that mathematical achievement is predicated on the development of students' number sense, spatial sense, data sense, and symbol sense. In other words, the development of mathematical power that entails using mathematical patterns and connections to make quantitative sense out of the world.

3. Many still believe that concepts and applications are fine, but can only be taught after students have developed a sound foundation of basic skills. Effective teachers increasingly believe that real-world situations and contexts (applications) and extensive work with concrete materials and pictorial representations (concept-building) are essential motivators for and prerequisites to skill development.

4. Many still believe that learning mathematics means memorizing an immutable set of basic skills. Effective teachers increasingly believe that "skills are to mathematics what scales are to music or spelling is to writing. The objective of learning is to write, to play music, or to

solve problems—not just to master skills. Practice with skills is just one of the many strategies used by good teachers to help students achieve the broader goals of learning" (*Everybody Counts*, p. 57).

5. Many still act on the belief that mathematics classes are best characterized by students working in isolation, passively using rote procedures to complete drill-and-practice exercises. Effective teachers increasingly act on the belief that mathematics classes are best characterized by students working in groups, actively engaged in solving engaging problems.

6. Many still act on the belief that students learn best when they are passive listeners, absorbers of written abstractions, and memorizers of procedures ("the rule for this is . . . ," "the formula for that is . . ."). Effective teachers increasingly act on the belief that students learn best when they are actively engaged by the context in which the mathematics is presented, and given frequent opportunities to discover and discuss.

7. Many still act on the belief that the primary goal of school mathematics is to prepare mathematicians and therefore, that mathematics should be abstract, rigorous, and accessible to only a few. Effective teachers act on the belief that, because school mathematics is part of universal education and because mathematical literacy is required for productive employment and an informed citizenry, sensible, useful mathematics must be made accessible to all students.

8. Many still believe that calculators and computers are unnecessary and potentially dangerous crutches that will impair the development of mathematical understanding. Effective teachers believe that calculators and computers are indispensable tools for broadening access to mathematical ideas, increasing student productivity, and enhancing the overall quality of instruction at all levels.

9. And perhaps most importantly, many still believe that mathematical ability is an innate characteristic and that many students just won't ever be successful in mathematics. Effective teachers believe and consistently act on the belief that *all* students can be successful in mathematics, that mathematical achievement is far more the result of effort than ability, and that it is the teacher who remains the critical variable for assuring student success.

Tomes of research speak of the effective instructor being a reflective instructor. Step back and reflect by asking yourself: What really are my beliefs? How are my actions consistent with my beliefs? How do my actions contradict my beliefs? Are my beliefs consistent with good practice? Which of my beliefs might I consider reconsidering?

This article first appeared in the *ATOMIC Journal*, Fall, 1989.

Dreams, Ideas, and Tools for Making Middle School Mathematics Really Work: Thoughts for The New Standards Project

Introduction

My charge in this task is not so very different from what we ask of teachers each day, week, and year: Be visionary, yet practical. Be true to the spirit of the NCTM standards, while recognizing that we must teach real kids, in real school environments, facing an often overwhelming set of constraints. Set high standards for both students and teachers (the vision), yet remain mindful of the limitations of time and the desperate need for support shared by both students and teachers (the reality). So let me wander from dreams to practical suggestions in an exploration of "What would *I* teach next year if I focus on balancing the vision and the reality?"

The Dream (Part 1)

Just imagine that all the textbooks disappeared. Just imagine that we made school interesting and engaging for most kids, most of the time. Just imagine that we believed that kids learn by doing and by constructing their own understanding, and that we actually acted on this belief. And just imagine that we simplified curriculum and instruction to those activities that fostered this vision.

Just imagine that a year of school meant

- reading, writing about, and discussing six or more works of fiction;
- reading, writing about, and discussing six or more works of nonfiction that related to the year's work in science, health, and/or social studies;
- keeping a daily journal;
- weekly creative writing opportunities;
- ongoing opportunities to create art, music, dance, and drama;

- daily independent, silent, sustained reading;
- ten or so AIMS-like science (with some math) units;
- eight or so integrated, thematic mathematics units;
- four quarter-long social studies investigations;
- two week-long cooperative group projects/investigations;
- one independent study project complete with report, display, and oral presentation; and
- weekly "current events" newspaper/magazine review/discussions to address history, health, civics, and other connections.

Sure I'm dreaming. But we ought to start by remembering that mathematics is not taught in a vacuum and that mathematics teachers depend deeply on their colleagues and on the school structures around them.

The Dream (Part 2)

And what do those "eight or so integrated, thematic mathematics units" look like? What follows is a rough vision with rough descriptions for possible three- to four-week units probably best suited for sixth grade. The units attempt to address the big ideas that I would expect sixth graders to be wrestling with by embedding them in mathematically rich and situationally engaging contexts.

Unit 1—Movie Theater: *ratio, proportion, angles, measurement, scale*
Students design and create scale drawings of their ideal movie theater. They discuss the various features of movie theaters and where mathematics is "hidden" in the design of such theaters. Students then use scale drawings and create their own scale drawings of the floor plans of several theaters of varying size and seating arrangements. Investigations with overhead projectors are used to explore viewing angles and the appropriate placement of the projector in a theater. Students also investigate slopes and angles by looking for the ideal slant of the floor. Finally, students explore the business aspects of running a theater, including scheduling of films and running the concession stand.

Unit 2—The Phantom Tollbooth: *language and logic, large numbers, averages, three-dimensional figures*
Students read *The Phantom Tollbooth* by Norton Juster with several time outs to discuss, study, and explore the varied mathematics embedded in the novel, including such ideas as the rounding and reasonableness of large numbers, the validity of logical arguments, the use and characteristics of various three-dimensional geometric shapes, and the use and abuse of measures of central tendency.

Unit 3—Round and Round the Pizza Parlor: *circles, circumference, area, measurement*

Students are launched into this unit with a question like: Given the choice of two 6 inch in diameter pizzas for $7.95 or one 9 inch in diameter pizza for $8.95, which gives the most pizza and which is the better buy? Students investigate various circles; tabulate data on diameter, radius, circumference; and estimate areas to discover the presence and role of π in working with circles. Unit activities include the generation of the formula for the area of a circle from an array of very thin pizza slices, an investigation of the reasonableness of the claim that Americans consume 100 acres of pizza daily, and explorations of how doubling and tripling a circle's diameter affects its circumference and its area.

Unit 4—The Carnival: *probability, fraction, percentage*

Students are shown several games of chance to play and to record data from. Analysis of results is used to develop a sense of likelihood of outcomes, fairness, and probability. For example, games to be created, played, and analyzed might include wheels of fortune or spinner games, rolling balls down numbered alleys in search of totals greater than a given number, and/or balloon-bursting dart games—so that students get to explore geometric as well as numeric situations. Again, working only experimentally (no empirical probability or expected value work) students can explore the pricing and reward structure for several games. This might also extend to the state lottery games of chance. Finally, working in groups, students design, create, and defend the price per try and prize structure for their carnival game.

Unit 5—Weird Buildings from Boxes, Cones, Tubes, and Pyramids: *three-dimensional shapes and spatial visualization*

Students use index card stock to create various sized models of rectangular prisms, cones, cylinders, and pyramids. They use these models to build definitions for these shapes and to describe them to "alien" creatures. Students will amass real-world instances of the occurrence of these shapes and describe why they are used (e.g., ice cream cone rather than ice cream cylinder, or rectangular prism box rather than pyramid-shaped container). Activities will then focus on measuring surface area and volume of these shapes. Finally, students will create a streetscape using their models and construct top and front two-dimensional views as well as a three-dimensional sketch of their "weird city block."

Unit 6—Salami, Balony, and Fractions: *fraction and mixed number equivalents, sums and differences of fractions, links to decimals, and relative magnitude*

Students are given a range of realistic delicatessen data because delis are settings where fractions and fraction-decimal relationships occur often and naturally (e.g., ¾ of a pound, 1.82 ounces). Using measuring (weights expressed as fractions) and pricing (prices expressed as rates), students engage in a range of activities designed to broaden and deepen their understanding of proportional reasoning, measuring, and measurement conversions. They also report results of investigations and display and analyze data. Specific activities should include exploration of the links between verbal orders and electronic scale displays (e.g., three-quarters of a pound and .73 pounds), investigations of unit prices and using unit prices to determine best buys, pricing schemes for different sizes of particular products, and the pros and cons of house brands versus national brands. Activities should also allow students to assume the role of customer as well as deli employee to focus on diverse uses of fractions. A culminating activity might be planning and ordering cold cuts, etc. for a party for *x* number of people.

Unit 7—So What's Our Opinion? *sampling, surveying, numerical equivalents*
Students study and interpret various survey findings and write headlines and the first several paragraphs of a release accompanying the report of the survey findings (see for example the findings for various phenomena in Poretz and Sinrod, "The First Really Important Survey of American Habits"). Students will then discuss how the selection of the sample could or couldn't have biased the results and how sampling can influence survey results. Using "cubes in a bag" experiments, students discover why sampling is necessary and formulate elementary notions of appropriate sample size. Students then create their own survey of fellow students on topics of interest to students, gather data from an unbiased sample, display and analyze the data, and report their findings. An additional focus of this unit is on numerical equivalents in reporting findings (e.g., 12 out of 25, a little less than $\frac{1}{2}$, about 50 percent all convey the same message).

Unit 8—Size and Shape in the Supermarket: *volume, weight, cost per unit, measurement, nutrition*
Students bring in a collection of boxes and cans of typical foodstuffs like cereal, rice, soup, corn, crackers, etc. Using the labels, intuition, and estimation, students carry out a range of activities that draw on diverse mathematical skills and understandings. For example, students should order the containers on a table from smallest to largest without first measuring. Then students should use rulers to find the actual volume of each container and discuss discrepancies between the original order and the actual order. Containers could also be ordered by weight. Additional activities include average cost per item, total cost of the boxes and cans, cost per ounce, cost per gram of protein, etc. Students conclude this unit by using the nutritional information on the label to "sell" their particular item— that is put it in the best light.

Unit 9—Same Shape, Different Size: *similarity*

Students begin with an inductive approach to similarity. They may see drawings of similar and dissimilar objects and then discuss what is the same and what is different about the objects—such things as triangles, rectangles, and circles, but also drawings or pictures of stars, nails, trees, etc. Then students use interesting drawings or photographs and scale them to different sizes using grids or coordinates. Through measuring as many characteristics of the drawings as possible, students come to discover which attributes do not vary with size changes and which do—leading to discussion and use of the notions of proportionality.

Unit 10—Winning Ways and Other Strategies: *discrete mathematics, strategy, logic*

Students play and analyze a wide variety of nim-type games and develop winning strategies. The goal is not to beat other students but the development of a sense of strategy independent of the particular opponent; that is, a strategy must work no matter what an opponent does. Students learn to recognize the salient attributes of positions in nim games and can analyze both positions in games and entire games.

Finally, for culminating projects, mini-units, or focused investigations, students would be expected to complete the following:

The Pancake Breakfast Project

The Catalog Ordering Project

The $10,000 Stock Market Spree Investigation

From Dreams to Reality

Unfortunately, most schools are not yet structured to allow for the first part of the dream, nor are the materials readily available to proceed with the second part of the dream. However, nothing stops us from closing our doors, teaming with our colleagues if we can, and cutting and pasting a powerful mathematics program out of what is currently available and under development.

For example, faced with the need to create a new course for eighth graders who had completed algebra in seventh grade, Judy Narveson, a teacher at Farmington, Connecticut's Irving Robbins Middle School, created a ten-unit course drawn from a broad array of resources:

1. Review of Algebra

2. "Growth Patterns"—Linear and Exponential Functions from the Investigations Mathematics Curriculum Project

3. "Flying Through Math"—Trigonometry and Vectors from Wings

4. "Data Analysis"—from the Quantitative Literacy materials

5. "Investigations in Geometry"—from the NCTM Geometry Addenda Book

6. "Probability"—from the Quantitative Literacy materials

7. "Mathematics and Medicine"—from Jansen's *Contemporary Applied Mathematics Materials*

8. "Matrices"—from Wings

9. "Linear Programming"—from Addison-Wesley's *Topics in Discrete Mathematics*

10. "Iterations and Fractals"—Chapter 12 in McDougal-Littel's *Gateways* text

Doing What Judy Did

To create a similar course for more typical middle school students, I'd begin with a clear sense of the big ideas for my grade level. I'd draw these from the NCTM Standards, the California Mathematics Framework, and the New Standards Project draft Content Standards. I'd focus on building a year's worth of mathematical experiences designed to help my students develop more powerful number sense, data sense, spatial sense, and symbol sense. I'd seek out materials that engage students in solving real problems, not just getting answers; that demand full explanations and justifications, not just solutions; and that foster real connections both within mathematics and with other disciplines, not isolate skills, concepts, and topics. I'd make sure they all had graphing calculators! I'd make sure that my choices include multiple opportunities to use numbers; to estimate; to explain what operation(s) to use and why; to explore multiple representations of each mathematical element; to measure and convert measurements; to develop proportional reasoning; to collect, display, and analyze data; to examine, explore, and generalize patterns; to investigate and generalize functional relationships; and to explore shape and dimension so that there was balance between and among the major strands of the curriculum. And then I'd pick and choose, cut and paste, try out and retry from among the many available resource materials for making middle school mathematics work.

In short, have fun, read the kids' faces, keep experimenting, and keep learning!

Selected Resources for Fostering Sensible Mathematics

No one can be expected to read everything. Therefore, I have selected thirteen resources that share a similar overall perspective of what mathematics programs should look like but that offer diverse perspectives on various aspects of a high-quality program. These thirteen resources would constitute an excellent professional library for anyone seeking to build excellent mathematics curriculum, instruction, and assessment.

1. *Everybody Counts: A Report to the Nation on the Future of Mathematics Education*, National Research Council, National Academy Press, Washington, DC, 1989.

   Although over a decade old, this 114-page gem is still the clearest and most compelling case for reforming mathematics education in the United States yet written.

2. *Principles and Standards for School Mathematics*, National Council of Teachers of Mathematics, Reston, VA, 2000.

   This is the updated, consolidated, and more coherent set of curriculum standards developed by NCTM to lead mathematics into the twenty-first century. Along with its electronic companion (see www.nctm.org), these standards provide a wealth of guidance, direction, and examples.

3. *Curriculum and Evaluation Standards for School Mathematics*, National Council of Teachers of Mathematics, Reston, VA, 1989, and *Professional Standards for Teaching Mathematics*, National Council of Teachers of Mathematics, Reston, VA, 1991.

   These are the original two sets of Standards that essentially launched the national movement toward educational standards. Despite the

2000 update, both the Evaluation Standards and the Standards for Teaching Mathematics continue to be important descriptions of what should be occurring within all mathematics programs.

4. *Making Change in Mathematics Education: Learning from the Field*, edited by Joan Ferrini-Mundy, et al., National Council of Teachers of Mathematics, Reston, VA, 1998.

This book summarizes the findings of the Recognizing and Recording Reform in Mathematics Education project and documents a qualitative study of seventeen sites around the country that were engaged in Standards-based change in mathematics teaching and learning. The findings are comforting to those wrestling with reform and informative for those about to embark on reform.

5. *Beyond Arithmetic: Changing Mathematics in the Elementary Classroom*, by Jan Mokros, et al., Dale Seymour Publications, Palo Alto, CA, 1995.

This highly readable account summarizes the beliefs, experiences, and findings of the primary developers of TERC's "Investigations in Number, Data and Space" curriculum materials as they developed and piloted these materials. Chapter 4, "Questions Teachers Ask," is particularly helpful.

6. *Putting It Together: Middle School Math in Transition*, by Gary Tsuruda, Heinemann, Portsmouth, NH, 1994.

Tsuruda's personal story of how and why one teacher changes provides unequalled insight into the dynamics of professional growth and changing instructional practices. Teachers find it easy to relate to Tsuruda's experiences.

7. *Mathematical Power: Lessons from a Classroom*, by Ruth E. Parker, Heinemann, Portsmouth, NH, 1993.

This book takes the reader into a fifth-grade classroom where Parker and her co-teacher are striving to make thinking and reasoning primary components of instruction. The lesson accounts and student dialogue provide a clear sense of what is meant by mathematical power and how it can be developed in all students.

8. *Constructive Assessment in Mathematics: Practical Steps for Teachers*, by David Clarke, Key Curriculum Press, Berkeley, CA, 1997.

This highly readable eighty-seven-page booklet outlines the elements of effective classroom assessment with clear guidance and practical examples.

9. *Why Numbers Count: Quantitative Literacy for Tomorrow's America,* edited by Lynn Arthur Steen, The College Board, New York, NY, 1997.

   One of the best sources of information on why and how the high school mathematics curriculum must be expanded and revised, the articles in this book make a strong case for a secondary mathematics curriculum that truly prepares students for the realities of the twenty-first century.

10. *Designing Professional Development for Teachers of Science and Mathematics,* by Susan Loucks-Horsley, et al., Corwin Press, Thousand Oaks, CA, 1998.

    This is a compendium of the best professional development practices, complete with strategies, discussion of critical issues and obstacles, and case studies. Anyone charged with providing professional development for teachers of mathematics will find the ideas and guidance in this book invaluable.

11. *Math: Facing an American Phobia,* by Marilyn Burns, Math Solutions Publications, Sausalito, CA, 1998.

    No one lays out the problems teachers face more directly than Marilyn Burns. This engaging and entertaining book takes on the fear of mathematics that so many—teachers included—have developed in school and provides an array of ideas for recrafting instruction in ways to minimize anxiety and maximize understanding.

12. *Leading the Way: Principals and Superintendents Look at Math Instruction,* edited by Marilyn Burns, Math Solutions Publications, Sausalito, CA, 1999.

    This book provides six diverse cases of how administrators worked to improve mathematics instruction in their school districts. Common threads are a clear vision of how children should learn mathematics and the need to support teachers throughout the change process. Principals and superintendents will find much of value here.

13. *TIMSS Moderator's Guide to Eighth-Grade Mathematics Lessons: United States, Japan, and Germany,* United States Department of Education, Washington, DC, 1997.

    This guide and the accompanying videotape of six lessons (two each from each of the three countries) constitute the *Teaching Module of Attaining Excellence: The TIMSS* (Third International Mathematics and Science Study) *Toolkit.* There are few resources that teachers find more compelling or that better initiate discussion and reflection on what typical mathematics instruction currently is and what it could be.

Additional Works Cited

The First Really Important Survey of American Habits. Mel Poretz and Barry Sinrod, Price Stern Sloan, Los Angeles, CA, 1989.

Pursing Excellence: A Study of U.S. Eighth-Grade Mathematics and Science Teaching, Learning, Curriculum, and Achievement in International Context. Lois Peak, U.S. Department of Education, National Center for Education Statistics, Washington, DC, 1996.